Trial and Triumph

Frances Ellen Watkins Harper

(Editor: Frances Smith Foster)

Alpha Editions

This edition published in 2024

ISBN : 9789362099648

Design and Setting By
Alpha Editions
www.alphaedis.com
Email - info@alphaedis.com

As per information held with us this book is in Public Domain.
This book is a reproduction of an important historical work. Alpha Editions uses the best technology to reproduce historical work in the same manner it was first published to preserve its original nature. Any marks or number seen are left intentionally to preserve its true form.

Contents

Chapter I .... - 1 -
Chapter II .... - 4 -
Chapter III .... - 8 -
Chapter IV .... - 12 -
Chapter V .... - 16 -
Chapter VI .... - 20 -
Chapter VII .... - 24 -
Chapter VIII .... - 28 -
Chapter IX .... - 33 -
Chapter X .... - 38 -
Chapter XI .... - 43 -
Chapter XII .... - 48 -
Chapter XIII .... - 52 -
Chapter XIV .... - 57 -
Chapter XV .... - 62 -
Chapter XVI .... - 67 -
Chapter XVII .... - 69 -
Chapter XVIII .... - 73 -
Chapter XIX .... - 78 -
Chapter XX .... - 83 -

Chapter I

"Oh, that child! She is the very torment of my life. I have been the mother of six children, and all of them put together, never gave me as much trouble as that girl. I don't know what will ever become of her."

"What is the matter now, Aunt Susan? What has Annette been doing?"

"Doing! She is always doing something; everlastingly getting herself into trouble with some of the neighbors. She is the most mischievous and hard-headed child I ever saw."

"Well what has she been doing this morning which has so upset you?"

"Why, I sent her to the grocery to have the oil can filled, and after she came back she had not been in the house five minutes before there came such an uproar from Mrs. Larkins', my next door neighbor, that I thought her house was on fire, but——"

"Instead of that her tongue was on fire, and I know what that means."

"Yes, that's just it, and I don't wonder. That little minx sitting up there in the corner looking so innocent, stopped to pour oil on her clean steps. Now you know yourself what an aggravating thing that must have been."

"Yes, it must have been, especially as Mrs. Larkins is such a nice housekeeper and takes such pride in having everything neat and nice about her. How did you fix up matters with her."

"I have not fixed them up at all. Mrs. Larkins only knows one cure for bad children, and that is beating them, and she always blames me for spoiling Annette, but I hardly know what to do with her. I've scolded and scolded till my tongue is tired, whipping don't seem to do her a bit of good, and I hate to put her out among strangers for fear that they will not treat her right, for after all she is very near to me. She is my poor, dead Lucy's child. Sometimes when I get so angry with her that I feel as though I could almost shake the life out of her, the thought of her dying mother comes back to me and it seems to me as if I could see her eyes looking so wistfully on the child and turning so trustingly to me and saying, 'Mother, when I am gone won't you take care of Annette, and try to keep her with you?' And then all the anger dies out of me. Poor child! I don't know what is going to become of her when my head is laid low. I'm afraid she is born for trouble. Nobody will ever put up with her as I do. She has such an unhappy disposition. She is not like any of my children ever were."

"Yes. I've often noticed that she does seem different from other children. She never seems light-hearted and happy."

"Yes, that is so. She reminds me so of poor Lucy before she was born. She even moans in her sleep like she used to do. It was a dark day when Frank Miller entered my home and Lucy became so taken up with him. It seemed to me as if my poor girl just worshiped him. I did not feel that he was all right, and I tried to warn my dear child of danger, but what could an old woman like me do against him with his handsome looks and oily tongue."

"Yes," said her neighbor soothingly, "you have had a sad time, but still we cannot recall the dead past, and it is the living present with which we have to deal. Annette needs wise guidance, a firm hand and a loving heart to deal with her. To spoil her at home is only to prepare her for misery abroad."

"I am afraid that I am not equal to the task."

"If any man lack wisdom we are taught to ask it of One who giveth liberally to all men and upbraideth none. There would be so much less stumbling if we looked earnestly within for 'the light which lighteth every man that cometh into the world.'"

"Well," said Mrs. Harcourt, Annette's grandmother, "there is one thing about Annette that I like. She is very attentive to her books. If you want to keep that child out of mischief just put a book in her hand; but then she has her living to get and she can't get it by nursing her hands and reading books. She has got to work like the rest of us."

"But why not give her a good education? Doors are open to her which were closed against us. This is a day of light and knowledge. I don't know much myself, but I mean to give my girls a chance. I don't believe in saying, let my children do as I have done, when I think some of us have done poorly enough digging and delving from morning till night. I don't believe the good Lord ever sent anybody into his light and beautiful world to be nothing but a drudge, and I just think it is because some take it so easy that others, who will do, have to take it so hard."

"It always makes my blood boil," said a maiden lady who was present, "to see a great hulk of a man shambling around complaining of hard times, and that he can't get work, when his wife is just working herself down to the grave to keep up the family." I asked Mrs. Johnson, who just lives in the wash tub and is the main stay of her family, what would her husband do if she were to die? and she said, 'get another wife.' Now, I just think she has spoiled that man and if she dies first, I hope that he will never find another woman to tread in her footsteps. He ought to have me to deal with. When he got through with me he would never want to laze around another woman."

"I don't think he ever would," said Mrs. Harcourt, while a gleam of humor sparkled in her eye. Her neighbor was a maiden lady who always knew how to manage other people's husbands, but had never succeeded in getting one of her own, and not having any children herself understood perfectly well how to rate other people's.

Just then a knock was heard at the door and Mr. Thomas, Annette's former school teacher, entered the room. After an exchange of courtesies he asked, "How does Annette come on with her new teacher?"

"I have not heard any complaint," said Mrs. Harcourt. "At first Mrs. Joseph's girl did not want to sit with Annette, but she soon got over it when she saw how well the other girls treated Annette and how pleasant the teacher was to her. Mr. Scott, who has been so friendly to us, told us not to mind her; that her mother had been an ignorant servant girl, who had married a man with a little money; that she was still ignorant, loud and [dressy?] and liked to put on airs. The nearer the beggar the greater the prejudice."

"I think it is true," said Mr. Thomas. "If you apply those words, not to condition, but human souls, for none but beggarly souls would despise a man because of circumstances over which he had no control; noble, large-hearted men and women are never scornful. Contempt and ridicule are the weapons of weak souls. I am glad however, that Annette is getting on so well. I hope that she will graduate at the head of her class, with high honors."

"What's the use of giving her so much education? there are no openings for her here, and if she gets married she won't want it," and Mrs. Harcourt sighed as she finished her sentence.

Mr. Thomas looked grave for a moment and then his face relaxed into a smile. "Well, really, Mrs. Harcourt, that is not very complimentary to us young men; do we have no need of intelligent and well educated wives? I think our race needs educated mothers for the home more than we do trained teachers for the school room. Not that I would ignore or speak lightly of the value of good colored teachers nor suggest as a race, that we can well afford to do without them; but to-day, if it were left to my decision, whether the education of the race should be placed in the hands of the school teacher or the mothers and there was no other alternative, I should, by all means, decide for the education of the race through its motherhood rather than through its teachers."

"But we poor mothers had no chance. We could not teach our children."

"I think you could teach some of them more than they wish to learn; but I must go now; at some other time we will talk on this subject."

Chapter II

"Oh, Annette!" said Mrs. Harcourt, turning to her granddaughter after Mr. Thomas had left the door; "What makes you so naughty? Why did you pour that oil on Mrs. Larkin's steps; didn't you know it was wrong?"

Annette stood silent looking like a guilty culprit.

"Why don't you answer me; what makes you behave so bad?"

"I don't know, grandma, I 'specs I did it for the devil. The preacher said the devil makes people do bad things."

"The preacher didn't say any such thing; he said the devil tempts people to be bad, but you are not to mind every thing the devil tells you to do, if you do, you will get yourself into a lot of trouble."

"Well, grandma, Mrs. Larkins is so mean and cross and she is always telling tales on me and I just did it for fun."

"Well, that is very poor fun. You deserve a good whipping, and I've a great mind to give it to you now."

"Why don't she let me alone; she is all the time trying to get you to beat me. She's a spiteful old thing anyhow. I don't like her, and I know she don't like me."

"Hush Annette, you must not talk that way of any one so much older than yourself. When I was a child I wouldn't have talked that way about any old person. Don't let me hear you talk that way again. You will never rest till I give you a good whipping."

"Yes ma'm," said Annette very demurely.

"Oh, Annette!" said her grandmother with a sudden burst of feeling. "You do give me so much trouble. You give me more worry than all my six children put together; but there is always one scabby sheep in the flock and you will be that one. Now get ready for school and don't let me hear any more complaints about you; I am not going to let you worry me to death."

Annette took up her bonnet and glided quietly out of the door, glad to receive instead of the threatened whipping a liberal amount of talk, and yet the words struck deeper than blows. Her own grandmother had prophesied evil things of her. She was to be the scabby sheep of the flock. The memory of the blows upon her body might have passed soon away after the pain and irritation of the infliction were over, but that inconsiderate prophecy struck deep into her heart and left its impress upon her unfolding life. Without intending it, Mrs. Harcourt had struck a blow at the child's self-respect; one of the things which she should have strengthened, even if it was "ready to die." Annette had entered life sadly handicapped. She was the deserted child of a selfish and unprincipled man and a young mother whose giddiness and lack of self-control had caused her to trail the robes of her womanhood in the dust. With such an ante-natal history how much she needed judicious, but tender, loving guidance. In that restless, sensitive and impulsive child was the germ of a useful woman with a warm, loving heart, ready to respond to human suffering, capable of being faithful in friendship and devoted in love. Before that young life with its sad inheritance seemed to lay a future of trial, and how much, humanly speaking, seemed to depend upon the right training of that life and the development within her of self-control, self-reliance and self-respect. There was no mother's heart for her to nestle upon in her hours of discouragement and perplexity; no father's strong, loving arms to shelter and defend her; no sister to brighten her life with joyous companionship, and no brother to champion her through the early and impossible period of ripening womanhood. Her grandmother was kind to her, but not very tender and loving. Her struggle to keep the wolf from the door had absorbed her life, and although she was neither hard nor old, yet she was not demonstrative in her affections, and to her a restless child was an enigma she did not know how to solve. If the child were hungry or cold she could understand physical wants, but for the hunger of the heart she had neither sympathy nor comprehension. Fortunately Annette had found a friend who understood her better than her grandmother, and who, looking beneath the perverseness of the child, saw in her rich possibilities, and would often speak encouragingly to her. Annette early developed a love for literature and poetry and would sometimes try to make rhymes and string verses together and really Mrs. Lasette thought that she had talent or even poetic genius and ardently wished that it might be cultivated and rightly directed; but it never entered the minds of her grandmother and aunts that in their humble home was a rarely gifted soul destined to make music which would set young hearts to thrilling with higher hopes and loftier aspirations.

Mrs. Lasette had been her teacher before she married. After she became a wife and mother, instead of becoming entirely absorbed in a round of household cares and duties, the moment the crown of motherhood fell upon her, as she often said, she had poured a new interest into the welfare of her race.[1] With these feelings she soon became known as a friend and helper in the community in which she lived. Young girls learned to look to her for council and encouragement amid the different passages of their [lives?] sometimes with blushing cheeks they whispered in to her ears tender secrets they did not always bring to their near relatives, and young men about to choose their life work, often came to consult her and to all her heart was responsive. With this feeling of confidence in her judgment, Mr. Thomas had entered her home after leaving Mrs. Harcourt's, educating himself for a teacher. He had spent several years in the acquisition of knowledge and was proving himself an acceptable and conscientious teacher, when the change came which deprived him of his school, by blending his pupils in the different ward schools of the city. Public opinion which moves slowly, had advanced far enough to admit the colored children into the different schools, irrespective of color, but it was not prepared, except in a few places to admit the colored teachers as instructors in the schools. "What are you going to do next?" inquired Mrs. Lasette of Mr. Thomas as he seated himself somewhat wearily by the fire. "I hardly know, I am all at sea, but I am going to be like the runaway slave who, when asked, 'Where is your pass?' raised his fist and said 'Dem is my passes,' and if 'I don't see an opening I will make one.'"

"Why don't you go into the ministry? When Mr. Pugh failed in his examination he turned his attention to the ministry, and it is said that he is succeeding admirably."

"Mrs. Lasette, I was brought up to respect the institutions of religion, and not to lay rash hands on sacred things, and while I believe that every man should preach Christ by an upright life, and chaste conversation, yet I think one of the surest ways to injure a Church, and to make the pulpit lose its power over the rising generation, is for men without a true calling, or requisite qualifications to enter the ministry because they have failed in some other avocation and find in preaching an open door to success."

"But they often succeed."

"How?"

"Why by getting into good churches, increasing their congregations and paying off large church debts." "And is that necessarily success? We need in the Church men who can be more than financiers and who can attract large congregations. We need earnest thoughtful Christly men, who will be more anxious to create and develop moral earnestness than to excite transient emotions. Now there is Rev. Mr. Lamson who was educated in R. College. I have heard him preach to, as I thought, an honest, well meaning, but an ignorant congregation, and instead of lifting them to more rational forms of worship, he tried to imitate them and made a complete failure. He even tried to moan as they do in worship but it didn't come out natural."

"Of course it did not. These dear old people whose moaning during service, seems even now so pitiful and weird, I think learned to mourn out in prayers, thoughts and feelings wrung from their agonizing hearts, which they did not dare express when they were forced to have their meetings under the surveillance of a white man."

"It is because I consider the ministry the highest and most sacred calling, that I cannot, nay I dare not, rush into it unless I feel impelled by the strongest and holiest motives."

"You are right and I think just such men as you ought to be in the ministry."

"Are you calling me?" "I wish it were in my power." "I am glad that it is not, I think there are more in the ministry now than magnify their calling."

"But Mr. Thomas[2] are you not looking on the dark side of the question? you must judge of the sun, not by its spots, but by its brightness."

"Oh I did not mean to say that the ministry is crowded with unworthy men, who love the fleece more than the flock. I believe that there are in the ministry a large number who are the salt of the earth and whose life work bears witness to their fitness. But unfortunately there are men who seem so lacking in reverence for God, by their free handling of sacred things; now I think one of the great wants of our people is more reverence for God who is above us, and respect for the man who is beside us, and I do hope that our next minister will be a good man, of active brain, warm heart and Christly sympathies, who will be among us a living, moral, and spiritual force, and who will be willing to teach us on the Bible plan of 'line upon line, precept upon precept, here a little there a little.'"

"I hope he will be; it is said that brother Lomax our new minister is an excellent young man."

"Well I hope that we will not fail to receive him as an apostle and try to hold up his hands."

"I hope so. I think that to be called of God to be an ambassador for Christ, to help him build the kingdom of righteousness, love and peace, amid the misery, sin and strife, is the highest and most blessed position that a man can hold, and because I esteem the calling so highly I would not rush into it unless I felt divinely commissioned."

Chapter III

Mrs. Harcourt was a Southern woman by birth, who belonged to that class of colored people whose freedom consisted chiefly in not being the chattels of the dominant race—a class to whom little was given and from whom much was required. She was naturally bright and intelligent, but had come up in a day when the very book of the Christian's law was to her a sealed volume; but if she had not been educated through the aid of school books and blackboards, she had obtained that culture of manners and behavior which comes through contact with well-bred people, close observation and a sense of self-respect and self-reliance, and when deprived of her husband's help by an untimely death, she took up the burden of life bravely and always tried to keep up what she called "a stiff upper lip." Feeling the cramping of Southern life, she became restive under the privations and indignities which were heaped upon free persons of color, and at length she and her husband broke up their home and sold out at a pecuniary sacrifice to come North, where they could breathe free air and have educational privileges for their children. But while she was strong and healthy her husband, whose health was not very firm, soon succumbed to the change of climate and new modes of living and left Mrs. Harcourt a stranger and widow in a strange land with six children dependent on her for bread and shelter: but during her short sojourn in the North[3] she had enlisted the sympathy and respect of kind friends, who came to her relief and helped her to help herself, the very best assistance they could bestow upon her. Capable and efficient, she found no difficulty in getting work for herself and older children, who were able to add their quota to the support of the family by running errands, doing odd jobs for the neighbors and helping their mother between school hours. Nor did she lay all the household burdens on the shoulders of the girls and leave her boys to the mercy of the pavement; she tried to make her home happy and taught them all to have a share in adding to its sunshine. "It makes boys selfish," she would say, "to have their sisters do all the work and let the boys go scot-free. I don't believe there would be so many trifling men if the boys were trained to be more helpful at home and to feel more for their mothers and sisters." All this was very well for the peace and sunshine of that home, but as the children advanced in life the question came to her with painful emphasis—
—"What can I do for the future of my boys and girls?" She was not anxious to have them all professional men and school teachers and government clerks, but she wanted each one to have some trade or calling by which a respectable and comfortable living could be made; but first she consulted their tastes and inclinations. Her youngest boy was very fond of horses, but instead of keeping him in the city, where he was in danger of getting too intimate with horse jockeys and stable boys, she found a place for him with an excellent farmer, who, seeing the tastes of the boy, took great interest in

teaching him how to raise stock and he became a skillful farmer. Her second son showed that he had some mechanical skill and ingenuity and she succeeded in getting him a situation with a first-class carpenter, and spared no pains to have him well instructed in all the branches of carpentry, and would often say to him, "John, don't do any sham work if you are going to be a carpenter; be thorough in every thing you do and try to be the best carpenter in A.P., and if you do your work better than others, you won't have to be all the time going around advertising yourself; somebody will find out what you can do and give you work." Her oldest son was passionately fond of books and she helped him through school till he was able to become a school teacher. But as the young man was high spirited and ambitious, he resolved that he would make his school teaching a stepping stone to a more congenial employment. He studied medicine and graduated with M.D., but as it takes a young doctor some time to gain the confidence of an old community, he continued after his graduation to teach and obtained a certificate to practice medicine. Without being forced to look to his mother for assistance, while the confidence of his community was slowly growing, he depended on the school for his living and looked to the future for his success as a physician.

For the girls, because they were colored, there were but few avenues open, but they all took in sewing and were excellent seamstresses, except Lucy, who had gone from home to teach school in a distant city as there were no openings of the kind for her at her own home.

Mrs. Harcourt was very proud of her children and had unbounded confidence in them. She was high-spirited and self-respecting and it never seemed to enter her mind that any evil might befall the children that would bring sorrow and shame to her home; but nevertheless it came and Lucy, her youngest child, the pet and pride of the household returned home with a great sorrow tugging at her heart and a shadow on her misguided life. It was the old story of woman's weakness and folly and man's perfidy and desertion. Poor child, how wretched she was till "peace bound up her bleeding heart," and even then the arrow had pierced too deep for healing. Sorrow had wasted her strength and laid the foundation of disease and an early death. Religion brought balm to the wounded spirit, but no renewed vigor to the wasted frame and in a short time she fell a victim to consumption, leaving Annette to the care of her mother. It was so pitiful to see the sorrow on the dear old face as she would nestle the wronged and disinherited child to her heart and would say so mournfully, "Oh, I never, never expected this!"

Although Annette had come into the family an unbidden and unwelcome guest, associated with the saddest experience of her grandmother's life, yet somehow the baby fingers had wound themselves around the tendrils of her heart and the child had found a shelter in the warm clasp of loving arms. To her, Annette was a new charge, an increased burden; but burden to be defended by her love and guarded by her care. All her other children had married and left her, and in her lowly home this young child with infantile sweetness, beguiled many a lonely hour. She loved Lucy and that was Lucy's child.

> But where was he who sullied
>   Her once unspotted name;
> Who lured her from life's brightness
>   To agony and shame?

Did society, which closed its doors against Lucy and left her to struggle as best she might out of the depth into which she had fallen, pour any righteous wrath upon his guilty head? Did it demand that he should at least bring forth some fruit meet for repentance by at least helping Mrs. Harcourt to raise the unfortunate child? Not so. He left that poor old grandmother to struggle with her failing strength, not only to bear her own burden, but the one he had so wickedly imposed upon her. He had left A.P. before Lucy's death and gone to the Pacific coast where he became wealthy through liquor selling, speculation, gambling and other disreputable means, and returned with gold enough to hide a multitude of sins, and then fair women permitted and even courted his society. Mothers with marriageable daughters condoned his offences against morality and said, "oh, well, young men will sow their wild oats; it is no use to be too straight laced." But there were a few thoughtful mothers old fashioned enough to believe that the law of purity is as binding upon the man as the woman, and who, under no conditions, would invite him to associate with their daughters. Women who tried to teach their sons to be worthy of the love and esteem of good women by being as chaste in their conversation and as pure in their lives as their young daughters who sat at their side sheltered in their pleasant and peaceful homes. One of the first things that Frank Miller did after he returned to A.P. was to open a large and elegantly furnished saloon and restaurant. The license to keep such a place was very high, and men said that to pay it he resorted to very questionable means, that his place was a resort for gamblers, and that he employed a young man to guard the entrance of his saloon from any sudden invasion of the police by giving a signal without if he saw any of them approaching, and other things were whispered of his saloon which showed it to be a far more dangerous place for the tempted, unwary and inexperienced feet of the young men of A.P., than any low groggery in the whole city. Young men who would have scorned to enter the lowest dens of vice, felt at home in his gilded palace of sin. Beautiful pictures adorned the walls, light streamed into the room through finely stained glass windows, women, not as God had made them, but as sin had debased them, came there to spend the evening in the mazy dance, or to sit with partners in sin and feast at luxurious tables. Politicians came there to concoct their plans for coming campaigns, to fix their slates and to devise means for grasping with eager hands the spoils of government. Young men anxious for places in the gift of the government found that winking at Frank Miller's vices and conforming to the demoralizing customs of his place were passports to political favors, and lacking moral stamina, hushed their consciences and became partakers of his sins.[4] Men talked in private of his vices, and drank his liquors and smoked his cigars in public. His place was a snare to their souls. "The dead were there but they knew it not." He built a beautiful home and furnished it magnificently, and some said that the woman who married him would do well, as if it were possible for any woman to marry well who linked her destinies to a wicked, selfish and base man, whose business was a constant menace to the peace, the purity and progress of society. I believe it was Milton who said that the purity of a man should be more splendid than the purity of a woman, basing his idea upon the declaration, "The head of the woman is the man, and the head of the man is Jesus Christ." Surely if man occupies this high rank in the creation of God he should ever be the true friend and helper of woman and not, as he too often proves, her falsest friend and basest enemy.

Chapter IV

"Annette," said Mrs. Harcourt one morning early, "I want you to stir your stumps to-day; I am going to have company this evening and I want you to help me to get everything in apple pie order."

"Who is coming, grandma?"

"Mr. Thomas and Mrs. Lasette."

"Mrs. Lasette!" Annette's eyes brightened. "I hope she will come; she is just as sweet as a peach and I do love her ever so much; and who else?"

"Brother Lomax, the minister who preached last Sunday and gave us such a good sermon."

"Is he coming, too?" Annette opened her eyes with pleased surprise. "Oh, I hope he will come, he's so nice."

"What do you know about him?"

"Why, grandmother, I understood everything that he said, and I felt that I wanted to be good just like he told us, and I went and asked aunt 'Liza how people got religion. She had been to camp-meeting and seen people getting religion, and I wanted her to tell me all about it for I wanted to get it too."

"What did she tell you?"

"She told me that people went down to the mourner's bench and prayed and then they would get up and shout and say they had religion, and that was all she knew about it."

"You went to the wrong one when you went to your aunt 'Liza. And what did you do after she told you?"

"Why, I went down in the garden and prayed and I got up and shouted, but I didn't get any religion. I guess I didn't try right."

"I guess you didn't if I judge by your actions. When you get older you will know more about it."

"But, grandma, Aunt 'Liza is older than I am, why don't she know?"

"Because she don't try; she's got her head too full of dress and dancing and nonsense."

Grandmother Harcourt did not have very much faith in what she called children's religion, and here was a human soul crying out in the darkness; but she did not understand the cry, nor look for the "perfecting of praise out of the mouths of babes and sucklings," not discerning the emotions of that young spirit, she let the opportunity slip for rightly impressing that young soul. She depended too much on the church and too little on the training of the home. For while the church can teach and the school instruct, the home is the place to train innocent and impressible childhood for useful citizenship on earth and a hope of holy companionship in heaven; and every Christian should strive to have "her one of the provinces of God's kingdom," where she can plant her strongest batteries against the ramparts of folly, sin and vice.

"Who else is coming, grandma?"

"Why, of course I must invite Mrs. Larkins; it would never do to leave her out."

Annette shrugged her shoulders, a scowl came over her face and she said:

"I hope she won't come."

"I expect she will and when she comes I want you to behave yourself and don't roll up your eyes at her and giggle at her and make ugly speeches. She told me that you made mouths at her yesterday, and that when Mr. Ross was whipping his horse you said you knew some one whom you wished was getting that beating, and she said that she just believed you meant her. How was that, Annette? If I were like you I would be all the time keeping this neighborhood in hot water."

Annette looked rather crestfallen and said, "I did make mouths at her house as I came by, but I didn't know that she saw me."

"Yes she did, and you had better mind how you cut your cards with her."

Annette finding the conversation was taking a rather disagreeable turn suddenly remembered that she had something to do in the yard and ceased to prolong the dialogue. If the truth must be confessed, Annette was not a very earnest candidate for saintship, and annoying her next door neighbor was one of her favorite amusements.

Grandma Harcourt lived in a secluded court, which was shut in on every side but one from the main streets, and her environments were not of the most pleasant and congenial kind. The neighbors, generally speaking, belonged to neither the best nor worst class of colored people. The court was too fully enclosed to be a thoroughfare of travel, but it was a place in which women could sit at their doors and talk to one another from each side of the court. Women who had no scruples about drinking as much beer, and sometimes stronger drinks, as they could absorb, and some of the men said that the women drank more than men, and under the besotting influence of beer and even stronger drinks, a fearful amount of gossiping, news-carrying and tattling went on, which often resulted in quarrels and contentions, which, while it never resulted in blood, sadly lowered the tone of social life. It was the arena of wordy strife in which angry tongues were the only weapons of warfare, and poor little Annette was fast learning their modes of battle. But there was one thing against which grandmother Harcourt set her face like flint, and that was sending children to saloons for beer, and once she flamed out with righteous indignation when one of her neighbors, in her absence, sent Annette to a saloon to buy her some beer. She told her in emphatic terms she must never do so again, that she wanted her girl to grow up a respectable woman, and that she ought to be ashamed of herself, not only to be guzzling beer like a toper, but to send anybody's child to a saloon to come in contact with the kind of men who frequented such places, and that any women who sent their children to such places were training their boys to be drunkards and their girls to be street-walkers. "I am poor," she said, "but I mean to keep my credit up and if you and I live in this neighborhood a hundred years you must never do that thing again."

Her neighbor looked dazed and tried to stammer out an apology, but she never sent Annette to a beer saloon again, and in course of time she became a good temperance woman herself, influenced by the faithfulness of grandmother Harcourt.

The court in which Mrs. Harcourt lived was not a very desirable place, but, on account of her color, eligible houses could not always be obtained, and however decent, quiet or respectable she might appear on applying for a house, she was often met with the rebuff, "We don't rent to colored people," and men who virtually assigned her race the lowest place and humblest positions could talk so glibly of the degradation of the Negro while by their Christless and inhuman prejudice they were helping add to their low social condition. In the midst of her unfavorable environments Mrs. Harcourt kept her home neat and tidy; sent Annette to school constantly and tried to keep her out of mischief, but there was moral contagion in the social atmosphere of Tennis Court and Annette too often succumbed to its influence; but Annette was young and liked the company of young girls and it seemed cruel to confine the child's whole life to the home and schoolhouse and give her no chance to be merry and playful with girls of her own age. So now and then grandmother Harcourt would let her spend a little time with some of the neighbors' girls but from the questions that Annette often asked her grandmother and the conversations she sometimes repeated Mrs. Harcourt feared that she was learning things which should only be taught by faithful mothers in hours of sacred and tender confidence, and she determined, even if it gave offence to her neighbors, that she would choose among her own friends, companions for her granddaughter and not leave all her social future to chance. In this she was heartily aided by Mrs. Lasette, who made it a point to hold in that neighborhood, mothers' meetings and try to teach mothers, who in the dark days of slavery had no bolts nor bars strong enough to keep out the invader from scattering their children like leaves in wintry weather, how to build up light and happy homes under the new dispensation of freedom. To her it was a labor of love and she found her reward in the peace and love which flowed into the soul and the improved condition of society. In lowly homes where she visited, her presence was a benediction and an inspiration. Women careless in their household and slatternly in their dress grew more careful in the keeping of their homes and the arrangement of their attire. Women of the better class of their own race, coming among them awakened their self-respect. Prejudice and pride of race had separated them from their white neighbors and the more cultured of their race had shrunk from them in their ignorance, poverty and low social condition and they were left, in a great measure, to themselves—ostracised by the whites on the one side and socially isolated from the more cultured of their race on the other hand. The law took little or no cognizance of them unless they were presented at its bar as criminals; but if they were neither criminals nor paupers they might fester in their vices and perpetuate their social condition. Who understood or cared to minister to their deepest needs or greatest wants? It was just here where the tender, thoughtful love of a warm-hearted and intelligent woman was needed. To her it was a labor of love, but it was not all fair sailing. She sometimes met with coldness and distrust where she had expected kindness and confidence; lack of sympathy where she had hoped to find ready and willing cooperation; but she knew that if her life was in harmony with God and Christly sympathy with man; for such a life there was no such word as fail.

Chapter V

By dint of energy and perseverance grandmother Harcourt had succeeded in getting everything in order when her guests began to arrive. She had just put the finishing touches upon her well-spread table and was reviewing it with an expression of pleasure and satisfaction. And now while the guests are quietly taking their seats let me introduce you to them.

Mr. Thomas came bringing with him the young minister, Rev. Mr. Lomax, whose sermon had so interested and edified Mrs. Harcourt the previous Sunday. Mrs. Lasette, looking bright and happy, came with her daughter, and Mrs. Larkins entered arrayed in her best attire, looking starched and prim, as if she had made it the great business of her life to take care of her dignity and to think about herself. Mrs. Larkins,[5] though for years a member of church, had not learned that it was unchristian to be narrow and selfish. She was strict in her attendance at church and gave freely to its support; but somehow with all her attention to the forms of religion, one missed its warm and vivifying influence from her life, and in the loving clasp of a helping hand, in the tender beam of a sympathizing glance, weary-hearted mothers and wives never came to her with their heartaches and confided to her their troubles. Little children either shrank from her or grew quiet in her presence. What was missing from her life was the magnetism of love. She had become so absorbed in herself that she forgot everybody else and thought more of her rights than her duties. The difference between Mrs. Lasette and Mrs. Larkins was this, that in passing through life one scattered sunshine and the other cast shadows over her path. Mrs. Lasette was a fine conversationalist. She regarded speech as one of heaven's best gifts, and thought that conversation should be made one of the finest arts, and used to subserve the highest and best purposes of life, and always regretted when it was permitted to degenerate into gossip and backbiting. Harsh judgment she always tried to modify, often saying in doubtful cases, "Had we not better suspend our judgments? Truly we do not like people to think the worst of us and it is not fulfilling the law of love to think the worst of them. Do you not know that if we wish to dwell in his tabernacle we are not to entertain a reproach against our neighbor, nor to back-bite with our lips and I do not think there is a sin which more easily besets society than this." "Speech," she would say, "is a gift so replete with rich and joyous possibilities," and she always tried to raise the tone of conversation at home and abroad. Of her it might be emphatically said, "She opened her mouth with wisdom and in her lips was the law of kindness."

The young minister, Rev. Mr. Lomax, was an earnest, devout and gifted young man. Born in the midst of poverty, with the shadows of slavery encircling his early life, he had pushed his way upward in the world, "toiling while others slept." His father was dead. While living he had done what he could to improve the condition of his family, and had, it was thought, overworked himself in the struggle to educate and support his children. He was a kind and indulgent father and when his son had made excellent progress in his studies, he gave him two presents so dear to his boyish heart— a gun and a watch. But the hour came when the loving hands were closed over the quiet breast, and the widowed wife found herself unable to provide the respectable funeral she desired to give him. Thomas then came bravely and tenderly to her relief. He sold his watch and gun to defray the funeral expenses of his father. He was a good son to his aged mother, and became the staff of her declining years. With an earnest purpose in his soul, and feeling that knowledge is power, he applied himself with diligence to his studies, passed through college, and feeling within his soul a commission to teach and help others to develop within themselves the love of nature, he entered the ministry, bringing into it an enthusiasm for humanity and love of Christ, which lit up his life and made him a moral and spiritual force in the community. He had several advantageous offers to labor in other parts of the country, but for the sake of being true to the heavenly vision, which showed him the needs of his people and his adaptation to their wants, he chose, not the most lucrative, but the most needed work which was offered him with

A joy to find in every station,
Something still to do or bear.

He had seen many things in the life of the people with whom he was identified which gave him intense pain, but instead of constantly censuring and finding fault with their inconsistencies of conscience, he strove to live so blamelessly before them that he would show them by example a more excellent way and "criticise by creation." To him religion was a reasonable service and he wished it to influence their conduct as well as sway their emotions. Believing that right thinking is connected with right living, he taught them to be conservative without being bigoted, and liberal without being morally indifferent and careless in their modes of thought. He wanted them to be able to give a reason for the faith that was in them and that faith to be rooted and grounded in love. He was young, hopeful, and enthusiastic and life was opening before him full of hope and promise.

"It has been a beautiful day," said Mrs. Lasette, seating herself beside Mrs. Larkins,[6] who always waited to be approached and was ever ready to think that some one was slighting her or ignoring her presence.

"It has been a fine day, but I think it will rain soon; I judge by my corn."

"Oh! I think the weather is just perfect. The sun set gloriously this evening and the sky was the brightest blue."

"I think the day was what I call a weather breeder. Whenever you see such days this time of year, you may look out for falling weather. I [expect?] that it will snow soon."

"How that child grows," said Mrs. Larkins, as Annette entered the room.

"Ill weeds grow apace; she has nothing else to do. That girl is going to give her grandmother a great deal of trouble."

"Oh! I do not think so."

"Well, I do, and I told her grandmother so one day, but she did not thank me for it."

"No, I suppose not."

"I didn't do it for thanks; I did it just to give her a piece of my mind about that girl. She is the most mischievous and worrisome child I ever saw. The partition between our houses is very thin and many a time when I want to finish my morning sleep or take an afternoon nap, if Mrs. Harcourt is not at home, Annette will sing and recite at the top of her voice and run up and down the stairs as if a regiment of soldiers were after her."

"Annette is quite young, full of life and brimful of mischief, and girls of that age I have heard likened to persimmons before they are ripe; if you attempt to eat them they will pucker your mouth, but if you wait till the first frost touches them they are delicious. Have patience with the child, act kindly towards her, she may be slow in developing womanly sense, but I think that Annette has within her the making of a fine woman."

"Do you know what Annette wants?"

"Yes, I know what she wants; but what do you think she wants?"

"She wants kissing."

"I'd kiss her with a switch if she were mine."

"I do not think it wise to whip a child of her age."

"I'd whip her if she were as big as a house."

"I do not find it necessary with my Laura; it is sufficient to deter her from doing anything if she knows that I do not approve of it. I have tried to establish perfect confidence between us. I do not think my daughter keeps a secret from me. I think many young persons go astray because their parents have failed to strengthen their characters and to forewarn and forearm them against the temptations and dangers that surround their paths. How goes the battle?" said Mrs. Lasette, turning to Mr. Thomas.

"I am still at sea, and the tide has not yet turned in my favor. Of course, I feel the change; it has taken my life out of its accustomed channel, but I am optimist enough to hope that even this change will result in greater good to the greatest number. I think one of our great wants is the diversification of our industries, and I do not believe it would be wise for the parents to relax their endeavors to give their children the best education in their power. We cannot tell what a race can do till it utters and expresses itself, and I know that there is an amount of brain among us which can and should be utilized in other directions than teaching school or seeking for clerkships. Mr. Clarkson had a very intelligent daughter whom he wished to fit for some other employment than that of a school teacher. He had her trained for a physician. She went to B., studied faithfully, graduated at the head of her class and received the highest medal for her attainments, thus proving herself a living argument of the capability in her race. Her friend, Miss Young, had artistic talent, and learned wood carving. She developed exquisite taste and has become a fine artist in that branch of industry. A female school teacher's work in the public schools is apt to be limited to her single life, but a woman who becomes proficient in a useful trade or business, builds up for herself a wall of defense against the invasions of want and privation whether she is married or single. I think that every woman, and man too, should be prepared for the reverses of fortune by being taught how to do some one thing thoroughly so as to be able to be a worker in the world's service, and not a pensioner upon its bounty. And for this end it does not become us as a race to despise any honest labor which lifts us above pauperism and dependence. I am pleased to see our people having industrial fairs. I believe in giving due honor to all honest labor, in covering idleness with shame, and crowning labor with respect."

Chapter VI

For awhile Mrs. Harcourt was busy in preparing the supper, to which they all did ample justice. In her white apron, faultless neck handkerchief and nicely fitting, but plain dress, Mrs. Harcourt looked the impersonation of contented happiness. Sorrow had left deep furrows upon her kindly face, but for awhile the shadows seemed to have been lifted from her life and she was the pleasant hostess, forgetting her own sorrows in contributing to the enjoyment of others. Supper being over, her guests resumed their conversation.

"You do not look upon the mixing of the schools as being necessarily disadvantageous to our people," said the minister.

"That," said Mr. Thomas, "is just in accordance to the way we adapt ourselves to the change. If we are to remain in this country as a component part of the nation, I cannot fail to regard with interest any step which tends toward our unification with all the other branches of the human race in this Western Hemisphere."

"Although," said Mrs. Lasette, "I have been educating my daughter and have felt very sorry when I have witnessed the disappointment of parents who have fitted their children for teachers and have seen door after door closed against them, I cannot help regarding the mixing of the schools as at least one step in a right direction."

"But Mrs. Lasette," said the minister, "as we are educated by other means than school books and blackboards, such as the stimulus of hope, the incentives of self-respect and the consensus of public opinion, will it not add to the depression of the race if our children are made to feel that, however well educated they may be or exemplary as pupils, the color of their skin must debar them from entering avenues which are freely opened to the young girls of every other nationality."

Mr. Thomas replied, "In considering this question, which is so much broader than a mere local question, I have tried to look beyond the life of the individual to the life of the race, and I find that it is through obstacles overcome, suffering endured and the tests of trial that strength is obtained, courage manifested and character developed. We are now passing through a crucial period in our race history and what we so much need is moral earnestness, strength of character and purpose to guide us through the rocks and shoals on which so many life barques have been stranded and wrecked."

"Yes," said Mrs. Lasette, "I believe that we are capable of being more than light-hearted children of the tropics and I want our young people to gain more persistence in their characters, perseverance in their efforts and that esprit de corps, which shall animate us with higher, nobler and holier purpose in the future than we have ever known in the past; and while I am sorry for the parents who, for their children's sake, have fought against the entailed ignorance of the ages with such humble weapons as the washboard, flat iron and scrubbing brush, and who have gathered the crumbs from the humblest departments of labor, still I feel with Mr. Thomas that the mixing of the schools is a stride in the march of the nation, only we must learn how to keep step in the progress of the centuries."

"I do not think that I fully comprehend you," Mr. Lomax replied.

"Let me explain. I live in the 19th Ward. In that Ward are not a half dozen colored children. When my husband bought the land we were more than a mile from the business part of the city, but we were poor and the land was very cheap and my husband said that paying rent was like putting money in a sinking fund; so he resolved, even if it put us to a little disadvantage, that he would buy the tract of land where we now live. Before he did so, he called together a number of his acquaintances, pointed out to them the tract of land and told them how they might join with him in planting a small hamlet for themselves; but except the few colored neighbors we now have, no one else would join with us. Some said it was too far from their work, others that they did not wish to live among many colored people, and some suspected my husband of trying either to take the advantage of them, or of agrandising himself at their expense, and I have now dear friends who might have been living comfortably in their own homes, who, to-day, are crowded in tenement houses or renting in narrow alleys and little streets."

"That's true," said Mrs. Larkins, "I am one of them. I wanted my husband to take up with your husband's offer, but he was one of those men who knew it all and he never seemed to think it possible that any colored man could see any clearer than he did. I knew your husband's head was level and I tried to persuade Mr. Larkins to take up with his offer, but he would not hear to it; said he knew his own business best, and shut me up by telling me that he was not going to let any woman rule over him; and here I am to-day, Larkins gone and his poor old widow scuffing night and day to keep soul and body together; but there are some men you couldn't beat anything into their heads, not if you took a sledge hammer. Poor fellow, he is gone now and I ought not to say anything agin him, but if he had minded me, I would have had a home over my head and some land under my feet; but it is no use to grieve over spilled milk. When he was living if I said, yes, he was always sure to say, no. One day I said to him when he was opposing me, the way we live is like the old saying, 'Pull Dick and pull devil,' and what do you think he said?"

"I don't know, I'm sure, what was it?"

"Why, he just looked at me and smiled and said, 'I am Dick.' Of course he meant that I was the other fellow."

"But," said Mrs. Lasette, "this is a digression from our subject. What I meant to say is this, that in our Ward is an excellent school house with a half score of well equipped and efficient teachers. The former colored school house was a dingy looking building about a mile and a half away with only one young school teacher, who had, it is true, passed a creditable examination. Now, when my daughter saw that the children of all other nationalities, it mattered not how low and debasing might be their environments, could enter the school for which her father paid taxes, and that she was forced either to stay at home or to go through all weathers to an ungraded school, in a poorly ventilated and unevenly heated room, would not such public inequality burn into her soul the idea of race-inferiority? And this is why I look upon the mixed school as a right step in the right direction."

"Taking this view of the matter I see the pertinence of your position on this subject. Do you know," continued Mr. Lomax,[7] his face lighting up with a fine enthusiasm, "that I am full of hope for the future of our people?"

"That's more than I am," said Mrs. Larkins very coldly. "When you have summered and wintered them as I have, you will change your tune."

"Oh, I hope not," he replied with an accent of distress in his voice. "You may think me a dreamer and enthusiast, but with all our faults I firmly believe that the Negro belongs to one of the best branches of the human race, and that he has a high and holy mission in the great drama of life. I do not think our God is a purposeless Being, but his ways are not as our ways are, and his thoughts are not our thoughts, and I dare not say 'Had I his wisdom or he my love,' the condition of humanity would be better. I prefer thinking that in the crucible of pain and apparent disaster, that we are held by the hand of a loving Father who is doing for us all, the best he can to fit us for companionship with him in the eternities, and with John G. Whittier, I feel:

> Amid the maddening maze of things
>   When tossed by storm and flood,
> To one fixed stake my spirit clings
>   I know that God is good.

"I once questioned and doubted, but now I have learned to love and trust in 'Him whom the heavens must receive till the time of the restitution of all things.' By this trust I do not mean a lazy leaning on Providence to do for us what we have ability to do for ourselves. I think that our people need more to be taught how to live than to be constantly warned to get ready to die. As Brother Thomas said, we are now passing through a crucial period of our history and what we need is life—more abundant life in every fibre of our souls; life which will manifest itself in moral earnestness, vigor of purpose, strength of character and spiritual progression."

"I do hope," said Mr. Thomas, "that as you are among us, you will impart some of your earnestness and enthusiasm to our young people."

"As I am a new comer here, and it is said that the people of A.P., are very sensitive to criticism, though very critical themselves and rather set and conservative in their ways, I hope that I shall have the benefit of your experience in aiding me to do all I can to help the people among whom my lot is cast."

"You are perfectly welcome to any aid I can give you. Just now some of us are interested in getting our people out of these wretched alleys and crowded tenement houses into the larger, freer air of the country. We want our young men to help us fight the battle against poverty, ignorance, degradation, and the cold, proud scorn of society. Before our public lands are all appropriated, I want our young men and women to get homesteads, and to be willing to endure privations in order to place our means of subsistence on a less precarious basis. The land is a basis of power, and like Anteus in the myth, we will never have our full measure of material strength till we touch the earth as owners of the soil. And when we get the land we must have patience and perseverance enough to hold it."

"In one of our Western States is a city which suggests the idea of Aladdin's wonderful lamp. Where that city now stands was once the homestead of a colored man who came from Virginia and obtained it under the homestead law. That man has since been working as a servant for a man who lives on 80 acres of his former section, and who has plotted the rest for the city of C."

"How did he lose it?"

"When he came from the South the country was new and female labor in great demand. His wife could earn $1.50 a day, and instead of moving on his land, he remained about forty miles away, till he had forfeited his claim, and it fell into the hands of the present proprietor. Since then our foresight has been developing and some months since in travelling in that same State, I met a woman whose husband had taken up a piece of land and was bringing it under cultivation. She and her children remained in town where they could all get work, and transmit him help and in a few years, I expect, they will be comfortably situated in a home owned by their united efforts."

Chapter VII

What next? was the question Mr. Thomas was revolving in his mind, when a knock was heard at his door, and he saw standing on the threshold, one of his former pupils.

"Well, Charley, how does the world use you? Everything going on swimmingly?"

"Oh, no indeed. I have lost my situation."

"How is that? You were getting on so well. Mr. Hazleton seemed to be perfectly satisfied with you, and I thought that you were quite a favorite in the establishment. How was it that you lost your place?"

"I lost it through the meanness of Mr. Mahler."

"Mr. Mahler, our Superintendent of public schools?"

"Yes, it was through him that I lost my situation."

"Why, what could you have done to offend him?"

"Nothing at all; I never had an unpleasant word with him in my life."

"Do explain yourself. I cannot see why he should have used any influence to deprive you of your situation."

"He had it in his power to do me a mean, low-life trick, and he did it, and I hope to see the day when I will be even with him," said the lad, with a flashing eye, while an angry flush mantled his cheek.

"Do any of the family deal at Mr. Hazleton's store? Perhaps you gave some of them offence through neglect or thoughtlessness in dealing with them."

"It was nothing of the kind. Mr. Mahler knew me and my mother. He knew her because she taught under him, and of course saw me often enough to know that I was her son, and so last week when he saw me in the store, I noticed that he looked very closely at me, and that in a few moments after he was in conversation with Mr. Hazleton. He asked him, 'if he employed a nigger for a cashier?' He replied, 'Of course not.' 'Well,' he said, 'you have one now.' After that they came down to the desk where I was casting up my accounts and Mr. Mahler asked, 'Is Mrs. Cooper your mother?' I answered, 'yes sir.' Of course I would not deny my mother. 'Isn't your name Charley?'[8] and again I answered, yes; I could have resorted to concealment, but I would not lie for a piece of bread, and yet for mother's sake I sorely needed the place.

"What did Mr. Hazleton say?"

"Nothing, only I thought he looked at me a little embarrassed, just as any half-decent man might when he was about to do a mean and cruel thing. But that afternoon I lost my place. Mr. Hazleton said to me when the store was about to close, that he had no further use for me. Not discouraged, I found another place; but I believe that my evil genius found me out and that through him I was again ousted from that situation and now I am at my wits end."

"But, Charley, were you not sailing under false colors?"

"I do not think so, Mr. Thompson. I saw in the window an advertisement, 'A boy wanted.' They did not say what color the boy must be and I applied for the situation and did my work as faithfully as I knew how. Mr. Hazleton seemed to be perfectly satisfied with my work and as he did not seek to know the antecedents of my family I did not see fit to thrust them gratuitously upon him. You know the hard struggle my poor mother has had to get along, how the saloon has cursed and darkened our home and I was glad to get anything to do by which I could honestly earn a dollar and help her keep the wolf from the door, and I tried to do my level best, but it made no difference; as soon as it was known that I had Negro blood in my veins door after door was closed against me; not that I was not honest, industrious, obliging and steady, but simply because of the blood in my veins."

"I admit," said Mr. Thomas, trying to repress his indignation and speak calmly, "that it was a hard thing to be treated so for a cause over which you had not the least control, but, Charley, you must try to pick up courage."

"Oh, it seems to me that my courage has all oozed out. I think that I will go away; maybe I can find work somewhere else. Had I been a convict from a prison there are Christian women here who would have been glad to have reached me out a helping hand and hailed my return to a life of honest industry as a blessed crowning of their labors of love; while I, who am neither a pauper nor felon, am turned from place after place because I belong to a race on whom Christendom bestowed the curse of slavery and under whose shadow has flourished Christless and inhuman caste prejudice. So I think that I had better go and start life afresh."

"No, Charley, don't go away. I know you could pass as a white man; but, Charley, don't you know that to do so you must separate from your kindred and virtually ignore your mother? A mother, who, for your sake, would, I believe, take blood from every vein and strength from every nerve if it were necessary. If you pass into the white basis your mother can never be a guest in your home without betraying your origin; you cannot visit her openly and crown her with the respect she so well deserves without divulging the secret of your birth; and Charley, by doing so I do not think it possible that however rich or strong or influential you may be as a white man, that you can be as noble and as true a man as you will be if you stand in your lot without compromise or concealment, and feel that the feebler your mother's race is the closer you will cling to it. Charley, you have lately joined the church; your mission in the world is not to seek to be rich and strong, but because there is so much sin and misery in the world by it is to clasp the hand of Christ through faith and try to make the world better by your influence and gladder and brighter by your presence."

"Mr. Thomas I try to be, and I hope I am a Christian, but if these prejudices are consistent with Christianity then I must confess that I do not understand it, and if it is I do not want it. Are these people Christians who open the doors of charitable institutions to sinners who are white and close them against the same class who are black? I do not call such people good patriots, let alone clear-sighted Christians. Why, they act as if God had done wrong in making a man black, and that they have never forgiven him and had become reconciled to the workmanship of his hands."

"Charley, you are excited just now, and I think that you are making the same mistake that better educated men than you have done. You are putting Christianity and its abuses together. I do think, notwithstanding all its perversions, and all the rubbish which has gathered around its simplicity and beauty, that Christianity is the world's best religion. I know that Christ has been wounded in what should have been the house of his friends; that the banner of his religion which is broad enough to float over the wide world with all its sin and misery, has been drenched with the blood of persecution, trampled in the mire of slavery and stained by the dust of caste proscription; but I believe that men are beginning more fully to comprehend the claims of the gospel of Jesus Christ. I am not afraid of what men call infidelity. I hold the faith which I profess, to be too true, too sacred and precious to be disturbed by every wave of wind and doubt. Amid all the religious upheavals of the Nineteenth Century, I believe God is at the helm, that there are petrifactions of creed and dogma that are to [be] broken up, not by mere intellectual speculations, but by the greater solvent of the constraining love of Christ, and it is for this that I am praying, longing and waiting. Let schoolmen dispute and contend, the faith for which I most ardently long and earnestly contend, is a faith which works by love and purifies the soul."

"Mr. Thomas, I believe that there is something real about your religion, but some of these white Christians do puzzle me awfully. Oh, I think that I will go. I am sick and tired of the place. Everything seems to be against me."

"No, Charley; stay for your mother's sake. I know a noble and generous man who is brave enough to face a vitiated public opinion, and rich enough to afford himself the luxury of a good conscience. I shall tell him your story and try to interest him in your behalf. Will you stay?"

"I certainly will if he will give me any chance to get my living and help my mother."

"It has been said that everything has two handles, and if you take it by the wrong handle it will be too hard to hold."

"I should like to know which is the right handle to this prejudice against color."

"I do not think that there is prejudice against color in this country."

"No prejudice against color!" said Charley Cooper,[9] opening his eyes with sudden wonder. "What was it that dogged my steps and shut door after door against me? Wasn't that prejudice against color?"

"Whose color, Charley? Surely not yours, for you are whiter than several of Mr. Hazleton's clerks. Do you see in your case it was not prejudice against color?"

"What was it, then?"

"It was the information that you were connected by blood with a once enslaved and despised people on whom society had placed its ban, and to whom slavery and a low social condition had given a heritage of scorn, and as soon as he found out that you were connected with that race, he had neither the manliness nor the moral courage to say, the boy is capable and efficient. I see no cause why he should be dismissed for the crimes of his white ancestors. I heard an eminent speaker once say that some people would sing, 'I can smile at Satan's rage, and face a frowning world,' when they hadn't courage enough to face their next door neighbor on a moral question."

"I think that must be the case with Mr. Hazleton."

"I once used to despise such men. I have since learned to pity them."

"I don't see what you find to pity in Mr. Hazleton, unless it is his meanness."

"Well, I pity him for that. I think there never was slave more cowed under the whip of his master than he is under the lash of public opinion. The Negro was not the only one whom slavery subdued to the pliancy of submission. Men fettered the slave and cramped their own souls, denied him knowledge and then darkened their own spiritual insight, and the Negro, poor and despised as he was, laid his hands upon American civilization and has helped to mould its character. It is God's law. As ye sow, so shall ye reap, and men cannot sow avarice and oppression without reaping the harvest of retribution. It is a dangerous thing to gather

> The flowers of sin that blossom
> Around the borders of hell."

Chapter VIII

"I never want to go to that school again," said Annette entering Mrs. Lasette's sitting room, throwing down her books on the table and looking as if she were ready to burst into tears.

"What is the matter now, my dear child? You seem to be all out of sorts."

"I've had a fuss with that Mary Joseph."

"Mary Joseph, the saloon-keeper's daughter?"

"Yes."

"How did it happen?"

"Yesterday in changing seats, the teacher put us together according to the first letter in our last names. You know that I, comes next to J; but there wasn't a girl in the room whose name begins with I, and so as J comes next, she put Mary Joseph and myself together."

"Ireland and Africa, and they were not ready for annexation?"

"No, and never will be, I hope."

"Never is a long day, Annette, but go on with your story."

"Well, after the teacher put her in the seat next to me she began to wriggle and squirm and I asked her if anything was biting her, because if there was, I did not want it to get on me."

"Oh, Annette, what a girl you are; why did you notice her? What did she say?"

"She said if there was, it must have got there since the teacher put her on that seat, and it must have come from me."

"Well, Mary Joseph knows how to scratch as well as you do."

"Yes, she is a real scratch cat."

"And what are you, my dear; a pattern saint?"

"No," said Annette, as the ruefulness of her face relaxed into a smile, "but that isn't all; when I went to eat my lunch, she said she wasn't used to eating with niggers. Then I asked her if her mother didn't eat with the pigs in the old country, and she said that she would rather eat with them than to eat with me, and then she called me a nigger and I called her a poor white mick."

"Oh, Annette, I am so sorry; I am afraid that trouble may come out of this fuss, and then it is so wrong and unlady-like for you to be quarrelling that way. Do you know how old you are?"

"I am almost fourteen years old."

"Where was the teacher all this time? Did she know anything about it?"

"No; she was out of the room part of the time, but I don't think she likes colored people, because last week when Joe Smith was cutting up in school, she made him get up and sit alongside of me to punish him."

"She should not have done so, but I don't suppose she thought for one moment how it looked."

"I don't know, but when I told grandma about it, Mrs. Larkins was in the room, and she said if she had done a child of hers so, she would have gone there and sauced her head off; but grandma said that she would not notice it; that the easiest way is the best."

"I think that your grandmother was right; but what did Joe say?"

He said that the teacher didn't spite him; that he would as lieve sit by me as any girl in school, and that he liked girls."

"A little scamp."

"He says he likes girls because they are so jolly."

"But tell me all about Mary Joseph."

"Well, a mean old thing, she went and told her horrid old father, and just as I was coming along he took hold of my arm and said he had heard that I had called his daughter, Miss Mary Joseph, a poor white mick and that if I did it again he would give me a good thrashing, and that for two pins he would do it then."

"What next?"

"I guess I felt like Mrs. Larkins does when she says her Guinea gets up. My Guinea was up but I was afraid to show it. Oh, but I do hate these Irish. I don't like them for anything. Grandmother says that an Irishman is only a negro turned wrong side out, and I told her so yesterday morning when she was fussing with me."

"Say, rather, when we were fussing together; I don't think the fault was all on her side."

"But, Mrs. Lasette, she had no business calling me a nigger."

"Of course not; but would you have liked it [any] better if she had called you a negro?"

"No; I don't want her to call me anything of the kind, neither negro nor nigger. She shan't even call me black."

"But, Annette, are you not black?"

"I don't care if I am, she shan't call me so."

"But suppose you were to say to Miss Joseph, 'How white your face is,' do you suppose she would get angry because you said that she looked white?"

"No, of course not."

"But suppose you met her hurrying to school, and you said to her, how red and rosy you look this morning, would that make her angry?"

"I don't suppose that it would."

"But suppose she would say to you, 'Annette, how black your face is this morning,' how would you feel?"

"I should feel like slapping her."

"Why so; do you think because Miss Joseph——"

"Don't call her Miss, she is so mean and hateful."

"But that don't hinder her from being Miss Joseph; If she is rude and coarse, that is no reason why I should not have good manners."

"Oh, Mrs. Lasette you are too sweet for anything. I wish I was like you."

"Never mind my sweetness; that is not to the point. Will you listen to me, my dear?"

"Of course I will. I could listen to you all night."

"Well, if it were not for signs there's no mistaking I should think you had a lot of Irish blood in your veins, and had kissed the blarney stone."

"No I haven't and if I had I would try to let——"

"Hush, my child; how you do rattle on. Do you think because Miss Joseph is white that she is any better than you are."

"No, of course not."

"But don't you think that she can see and hear a little better than you can?"

"Why, no; what makes you ask such a funny question?"

"Never mind, just answer me a few more questions. Don't you think if you and she had got to fighting that she would have whipped you because she is white?"

"Why, of course not. Didn't she try to get the ruler out of my hand and didn't because I was stronger."

"But don't you think she is smarter than you are and gets her lessons better."

"Now you are shouting."

"Why, Annette, where in the world did you get that slang?"

"Why, Mrs. Lasette, I hear the boys saying it in the street, and the girls in Tennis Court all say it, too. Is there any harm in it?"

"It is slang, my child, and a young lady should never use slang. Don't use it in private and you will not be apt to use it in public. However humble or poor a person may be, there is no use in being coarse and unrefined."

"But what harm is there in it?"

"I don't say that there is any, but I don't think it nice for young ladies to pick up all sorts of phrases in the street and bring them into the home. The words may be innocent in themselves, but they may not have the best associations, and it is safer not to use them. But let us return to Miss Joseph. You do not think that she can see or hear any better than you can, learn her lessons any quicker than you can, and when it comes to a trial of strength that she is stronger than you are, now let me ask you one more question. Who made Miss Joseph?"

"Why, the Lord, of course."

"And who made you?"

"He made me, too."

"Are you sure that you did not make yourself?"

"Why, of course not," said Annette with an accent of wonder in her voice.

"Does God ever make any mistakes?"

"Why, no!"

"Then if any one calls you black, why should you get angry? You say it would not make Miss Joseph angry to say she looked white, or red and rosy."

"I don't know; I know I don't like it and it makes me mad."

"Now, let me explain the reason why it makes you angry to be called black. Suppose I were to burn my hand in that stove, what would I have on my hand?"

"A sore place."

"If it were your hand, what would you do?"

"I would put something on it, wrap it up to keep from getting cold into it and try to get it well as soon as I could."

"Well, that would be a very sensible way of dealing with it. In this country, Annette, color has been made a sore place; it has been associated with slavery, poverty and ignorance. You cannot change your color, but you can try to change the association connected with our complexions. Did slavery force a man to be servile and submissive? Learn to hold up your head and respect yourself. Don't notice Mary Joseph's taunts; if she says things to tease you don't you let her see that she has succeeded. Learn to act as if you realized that you were born into this world the child of the Ruler of the universe, that this is his world and that you have as much right in it as she has. I think it was Gilbert Haven, a Bishop of the Methodist Episcopal Church, a man for whose tombstone I do not think America has any marble too white or any laurel too green, who saw on his travels a statue of Cleopatra, which suggested to him this thought, 'I am black, but comely, the sun has looked down upon me, but I will make you who despise me feel that I am your superior,' and, Annette, I want you to be so noble, true and pure that if everybody should hate you, that no one could despise you. No, Annette, if Miss Joseph ever attempts to quarrel with you don't put yourself on the same level by quarreling with her. I knew her parents when they were very poor; when a half dozen of them slept in one room. He has made money by selling liquor; he is now doing business in one of the most valuable pieces of property I see in East L street. He has been a curse, and his saloon a nuisance in that street. He has gone up in property and even political influence, but oh, how many poor souls have gone down, slain by strong drink and debauchery."

Chapter IX

True to his word, Mr. Thomas applied to Mr. Hastings, the merchant, of whom he had spoken to his young friend. He went to his counting-room and asked for a private interview, which was readily granted. They had kindred intellectual and literary tastes and this established between them a free masonry of mind which took no account of racial differences.

"I have a favor to ask," said Mr. Thomas, "can you spare me a few moments?"

"I am at your service," Mr. Hasting replied, "what can I do for you?"

"I have," he said, "a young friend who is honest and industrious and competent to fill the place of clerk or cashier in your store. He has been a cashier for Hazleton & Co., and while there gave entire satisfaction."

"Why did he leave?"

"I cannot say, because he was guilty of a skin not colored like your own, but because a report was brought to Mr. Hazleton that he had Negro blood in his veins."

"And what then?"

"He summarily dismissed him."

"What a shame!"

"Yes, it was a shame, but this pride of caste dwarfs men's moral perception so that it prepares them to do a number of contemptible things which, under other circumstances, they would scorn to do."

"Yes, it is so, and I am sorry to see it."

"There are men, Mr. Hastings, who would grow hotly indignant if you would say that they are not gentlemen who would treat a Negro in a manner which would not be recognized as fair, even by ruffians of the ring, for, I believe, it is their code of honor not to strike a man when he is down; but with respect to the colored man, it seems to be a settled policy with some not only to push him down, but to strike him when he is down. But I must go; I came to ask a favor and it is not right to trespass on your time."

"No; sit still. I have a little leisure I can give you. My fall trade has not opened yet and I am not busy. I see and deplore these things of which you complain, but what can be done to help it?"

"Mr. Hastings, you see them, and I feel them, and I fear that I am growing morbid over them, and not only myself, but other educated men of my race, and that, I think, is a thing to be deprecated. Between the white people and the colored people of this country there is a unanimity of interest and I know that our interests and duties all lie in one direction. Can men corrupt and intimidate voters in the South without a reflex influence being felt in the North? Is not the depression of labor in the South a matter of interest to the North? You may protect yourself from what you call the pauper of Europe, but you will not be equally able to defend yourself from the depressed laborer of the new South, and as an American citizen, I dread any turn of the screw which will lower the rate of wages here; and I like to feel as an American citizen that whatever concerns the nation concerns me. But I feel that this prejudice against my race compresses my soul, narrows my political horizon and makes me feel that I am an alien in the land of my birth. It meets me in the church, it confronts me in business and I feel its influence in almost every avenue of my life."

"I wish, Mr. Thomas, that some of the men who are writing and talking about the Negro problem would only come in contact with the thoughtful men of your race. I think it would greatly modify their views."

"Yes, you know us as your servants. The law takes cognizance of our crimes. Your charitable institutions of our poverty, but what do any of you know of our best and most thoughtful men and women? When we write how many of you ever read our books and papers or give yourselves any trouble to come near us as friends and help us? Even some of your professed Christians are trying to set us apart as if we were social lepers."

"You draw a dark picture. I confess that I feel pained at the condition of affairs in the South, but what can we do in the South?"

"Set the South a better example. But I am hindering you in your business."

"Not at all. I want to see things from the same standpoint that you do."

"Put yourself then in my place. You start both North and South from the premise that we are an inferior race and as such you have treated us. Has not the consensus of public opinion said for ages, 'No valor redeems our race, no social advancement nor individual development wipes off the ban which clings to us'; that our place is on the lowest round of the social ladder; that at least, in part of the country we are too low for the equal administrations of religion and the same dispensations of charity and a fair chance in the race of life?"

"You bring a heavy verdict against us. I hardly think that it can be sustained. Whatever our motives may have been, we have been able to effect in a few years a wonderful change in the condition of the Negro. He has freedom and enfranchisement and with these two great rights he must work out his social redemption and political solution. If his means of education have been limited, a better day is dawning upon him. Doors once closed against him in the South are now freely opened to him, and I do not think that there ever was a people who freed their slaves who have given as much for their education as we have, and my only hope is that the moral life of the race will keep pace with its intellectual growth. You tell me to put myself in your place. I think if I were a colored young man that I would develop every faculty and use every power which God had given me for the improvement and development of my race. And who among us would be so blind and foolish as to attempt to keep down an enlightened people who were determined to rise in the scale of character and condition? No, Mr. Thomas, while you blame us for our transgressions and shortcomings, do not fail to do all you can to rouse up all the latent energies of your young men to do their part worthily as American citizens and to add their quota to the strength and progress of the nation."

"I am conscious of the truth and pertinence of your remarks, but bear with me just a few moments while I give an illustration of what I mean."

"Speak on, I am all attention. The subject you bring before me is of too vital importance to be constantly ignored."

"I have a friend who is presiding elder in the A.M.E. Church and his wife, I think, is capable of being a social and intellectual accession in any neighborhood in which they might live. He rented a house in the city of L. and being of a fair complexion I suppose the lessee rented to him without having a suspicion of his race connection. When it was ascertained that he and his family were colored, he was ordered to leave, and this man, holding among the ministers of that city the position of ambassador for Christ, was ordered out of the house on account of the complexion of his family. Was there not a screw loose in the religious sentiment of that city which made such an act possible? A friend of mine who does mission work in your city, some time since, found a young woman in the slums and applied at the door of a midnight mission for fallen women, and asked if colored girls could be received, and was curtly answered, 'no.' For her in that mission there was no room. The love of Christ constrained no hand to strive to rescue her from the depths of degradation. The poor thing went from bad to worse till at last, wrecked and blighted, she went down to an early grave the victim of strong drink. That same lady found on her mission a white girl; seeing a human soul adrift, regardless of color, she went, in company with some others, to that same mission with the poor castaway; to her the door was opened without delay and ready admittance granted. But I might go on reciting such instances until you would be weary of hearing and I of relating them; but I appeal to you as a patriot and Christian, is it not fearfully unwise to keep alive in freedom the old animosities of slavery? To-day the Negro shares citizenship with you. He is not arraying himself against your social order; his hands are not dripping with dynamite, nor is he waving in your face the crimson banners of anarchy, but he is increasing in numbers and growing in intelligence, and is it not madness and folly to subject him to social and public inequalities, which are calculated to form and keep alive a hatred of race as a reaction against pride of caste?"

"Mr. Thomas, you have given me a new view of the matter. To tell you the truth, we have so long looked upon the colored man as a pliable and submissive being that we have never learned to look at any hatred on his part as an element of danger, and yet I should be sorry to know that by our Southern supineness we were thoughtlessly helping create a black Ireland in our Gulf States, that in case the fires of anarchy should ever sweep through our land, that a discontented and disaffected people in our midst might be as so much fuel to fire."

"But really I have been forgetting my errand. Have you any opening in your store for my young friend?"

"I have only one vacancy, and that is the place of a utility man."

"What are the duties of that position?"

"Almost anything that comes to hand; tying up bundles, looking after the mails, scattering advertisements. A factotum whose work lies here, there and everywhere."

"I am confident that he will accept the situation and render you faithful service."

"Well, then send him around tomorrow and if there is anything in him I may be able to do better by him when the fall trade opens."

And so Charley Cooper was fortunate enough in his hour of perplexity to find a helping hand to tide him over a difficult passage in his life. Gratefully and faithfully did he serve Mr. Hastings, who never regretted the hour when he gave the struggling boy such timely assistance. The discipline of the life through which he was passing as the main stay of his mother, matured his mind and imparted to it a thoughtfulness past his years. Instead of wasting his time in idle and pernicious pleasure, he learned how to use his surplus dollar and how to spend his leisure hours, and this knowledge told upon his life and character. He was not very popular in society. Young men with cigars in their mouths and the perfume of liquor on their breaths, shrugged their shoulders and called him a milksop because he preferred the church and Sunday school to the liquor saloon and gambling dens. The society of P. was cut up and divided into little sets and coteries; there was an amount of intelligence among them, but it ran in narrow grooves and scarcely one[10] intellect seemed to tower above the other, and if it did, no people knew better how to ignore a rising mind than the society people of A.P. If the literary aspirant did not happen to be of their set. As to talent, many of them were pleasant and brilliant conversationalists, but in the world of letters scarcely any of them were known or recognized outside of their set. They had leisure, a little money and some ability, but they lacked the perseverance and self-denial necessary to enable them to add to the great resources of natural thought. They had narrowed their minds to the dimensions of their set and were unprepared to take expansive[11] views of life and duty. They took life as a holiday and the lack of noble purposes and high and holy aims left its impress upon their souls and deprived them of that joy and strength which should have crowned their existence and given to their lives its "highest excellence and beauty."

Chapter X

Two years have elapsed since we left Annette recounting her school grievances to Mrs. Lasette. She has begun to feel the social contempt which society has heaped upon the colored people, but she has determined not to succumb to it. There is force in the character of that fiery, impetuous and impulsive girl, and her school experience is bringing it out. She has been bending all her mental energies to compete for the highest prize at the commencement of her school, from which she expects to graduate in a few weeks. The treatment of the saloon-keeper's daughter, and that of other girls of her ilk, has stung her into strength. She feels that however despised her people may be, that a monopoly of brains has not been given to the white race. Mr. Thomas has encouraged her efforts, and taught her to believe that not only is her own honor at stake as a student, but that as a representative of her branch of the human race, she is on the eve of winning, or losing, not only for herself, but for others. This view of the matter increases her determination and rouses up all the latent energies of her nature, and she labors day and night to be a living argument of the capability in her race. For other girls who will graduate in that school, there will be open doors, and unclosed avenues, while she knows that the color of her skin will bar against her the doors of workshops, factories and school rooms, and yet Mr. Thomas, knowing all the discouragements around her path, has done what he could to keep her interest in her studies from flagging. He knows that she has fine abilities, but that they must be disciplined by trial and endeavor before her life can be rounded by success and triumph. He has seen several of her early attempts at versification; pleased and even delighted with them, he has shown them to a few of his most intellectual friends. Eager and earnest for the elevation of the colored people, he has been pained at the coldness with which they have been received.

"I do not call that poetry," said one of the most intelligent women of A.P.

"Neither do I see anything remarkable about her," said another.

"I did not," said Mr. Thomas, "bring you the effusions of an acknowledged poet, but I think that the girl has fine ability, which needs encouragement and recognition."

But his friends could not see it; they were very charry of their admiration, lest their judgment should be found at fault, and then it was so much easier to criticise than it was to heartily admire; and they knew it seemed safer to show their superior intelligence by dwelling on the defects, which would necessarily have an amount of crudeness in them than to look beneath the defects for the suggestions of beauty, strength and grace which Mr. Thomas saw in these unripe, but promising effusions. It seemed perfectly absurd with the surroundings of Tennis Court to expect anything grand or beautiful [to] develop in its midst; but with Annette, poetry was a passion born in her soul, and it was as natural for her to speak in tropes and figures as it was for others to talk in plain, common prose. Mr. Thomas called her "our inveterate poet," and encouraged her, but the literary aspirants took scarcely any interest in the girl whom they left to struggle on as best she might. In her own home she was doomed to meet with lack of encouragement and appreciation from her relatives and grandmother's friends. One day her aunt, Eliza Hanson, was spending the day with her mother, and Annette showed her some of her verses and said to her, "that is one of my best pieces."

"Oh, you have a number of best pieces," said her aunt, carelessly. "Can you cook a beefsteak?"

"I suppose I could if I tried."

"Well, you had better try than to be trying to string verses together. You seem to think that there must be something very great about you. I know where you want to get. You want to get among the upper tens, but you haven't got style enough about you for that."

"That's just what I tell her," said her grandmother. "She's got too many airs for a girl in her condition. She talks about writing a book, and she is always trying to make up what she calls poetry. I expect that she will go crazy some of these days. She is all the time talking to herself, and I just think it is a sin for her to be so much taken up with her poetry."

"You had better put her to work; had she not better go out to service?"

"No, I am going to let her graduate first."

"What's the use of it? When she's through, if she wants to teach, she will have to go away."

"Yes, I know that, but Mrs. Lasette has persuaded me to let Annette graduate, and I have promised that I would do so, and besides I think to take Annette from school just now would almost break her heart."

"Well, mother, that is just like you; you will work yourself almost to death to keep Annette in school, and when she is through what good will it do her?"

"Maybe something will turn up that you don't see just now. When a good thing turns up if a person ain't ready for it they can't take hold of it."

"Well, I hope a good husband will turn up for my Alice."

"But maybe the good husband won't turn up for Annette."

"That is well said, for they tell me that Annette is not very popular, and that some of the girls are all the time making fun of her."

"Well, they had better make fun of themselves and their own bad manners. Annette is poor and has no father to stand by her, and I cannot entertain like some of their parents can, but Annette, with all her faults, is as good as any of them. Talk about the prejudice of the white people, I think there is just as much prejudice among some colored as there is among them, only we do not get the same chance to show it; we are most too mixed up and dependent on one another for that." Just then Mrs. Lasette entered the room and Mrs. Hanson, addressing her, said, "We were just discussing Annette's prospects. Mother wants to keep Annette at school till she graduates, but I think she knows enough now to teach a country school and it is no use for mother to be working as she does to keep Annette in school for the sake of letting her graduate. There are lots of girls in A.P. better off than she who have never graduated, and I don't see that mother can afford to keep Annette at school any longer."

"But, Eliza, Annette is company for me and she does help about the house."

"I don't think much of her help; always when I come home she has a book stuck under her nose."

"Annette," said Mrs. Lasette, "is a favorite of mine; I have always a warm place in my heart for her, and I really want to see the child do well. In my judgment I do not think it advisable to take her from school before she graduates. If Annette were indifferent about her lessons and showed no aptitude for improvement I should say as she does not appreciate education enough to study diligently and has not aspiration enough to keep up with her class, find out what she is best fitted for and let her be instructed in that calling for which she is best adapted."

"I think," said Mrs. Hanson, "you all do wrong in puffing up Annette with the idea that she is something extra. You think, Mrs. Lasette, that there is something wonderful about Annette, but I can't see it, and I hear a lot of people say she hasn't got good sense."

"They do not understand the child."

"They all say that she is very odd and queer and often goes out into the street as if she never saw a looking glass. Why, Mrs. Miller's daughter just laughed till she was tired at the way Annette was dressed when she went to call on an acquaintance of hers. Why, Annette just makes herself a perfect laughing stock."

"Well, I think Mary Miller might have found better employment than laughing at her company."

"Now, let me tell you, Mary Miller don't take her for company, and that very evening Annette was at my house, just next door, and when Mary Miller went to church she never asked her to go along with her, although she belongs to the same church."

"I am sorry to say it," said grandmother Harcourt, "but your Alice hardly ever comes to see Annette, and never asks her to go anywhere with her, but may be in the long run Annette will come out better than some who now look down upon her. It is a long road that has no turn and Annette is like a singed cat; she is better than she looks."

"I think," said Mrs. Lasette, "while Annette is very bright and intelligent as a pupil, she has been rather slow in developing in some other directions. She lacks tact, is straightforward to bluntness and has not any style about her and little or no idea of company manners, but she is never coarse nor rude. I never knew her to read a book whose author I would blush to name, and I never heard her engage in any conversation I would shrink to hear repeated. I don't think there is a girl of purer lips in A.P. than Annette, and I do not think your set, as you call it, has such a monopoly of either virtue or intelligence that you can afford to ridicule and depress any young soul who does not happen to come up to your social standard. Where dress and style are passports Annette may be excluded, but where brain and character count Annette will gain admittance. I fear," said Mrs. Lasette, rising to go, "that many a young girl has gone down in the very depths who might have been saved if motherly women, when they saw them unloved and lonely, had reached out to them a helping hand and encouraged them to live useful and good lives. We cry am I my sister's keeper? [I?] will not wipe the blood off our hands if through pride and selfishness we have stabbed by our neglect souls we should have helped by our kindness. I always feel for young girls who are lonely and neglected in large cities and are in danger of being ensnared by pretended sympathies and false friendship, and, to-day, no girl is more welcome at any social gathering than Annette."

"Mrs. Lasette," said Mrs. Hanson, "you are rich and you can do as you choose in A.P. You can set the fashion."

"No; I am not rich, but I hope that I will always be able to lend a hand to any lonely girl who is neglected, slighted and forgotten while she is trying to do right, who comes within my reach while I live in A.P. Good morning."

"Annette," said Mrs. Hanson,[12] "has a champion who will stand by her."

"Yes," said Mrs. Harcourt,[13] "Anna is true as steel; the kind of woman you can tie to. When my great trouble came, she was good as gold, and when my poor heart was almost breaking, she always had a kind word for me. I wish we had ten thousand like her."

"Well, mother, I must go, but if Annette does graduate don't let her go on the stage looking like a fright. General H's daughter has a beautiful new silk dress and a lovely hat which she got just a few weeks before her mother's death; as she has gone in black she wants to sell it, and if you say so, and will pay for it on installments, I can get if for Annette, and I think with a little alteration it would be splendid for her graduation dress."

"No; Eliza, I can't afford it."

"Why, mother, Annette will need something nice for the occasion, and it will not cost any more than what you intend to pay for her dress and hat. Why not take them?"

"Because Annette is not able to wear them. Suppose she had that one fine dress and hat, would she not want more to match with them? I don't want her to learn to dress in a style that she cannot honestly afford. I think this love of dress is the ruination of many a young girl. I think this straining after fine things when you are not able to get them, is perfectly ridiculous. I believe in cutting your coat according to your cloth. I saw Mrs. Hempstead's daughter last Sunday dressed up in a handsome light silk, and a beautiful spring hat, and if she or her mother would get sick to-morrow, they would, I suppose, soon be objects of public charity or dependent on her widowed sister, who is too proud to see her go to the poor house; and this is just the trouble with a lot of people; they not only have their own burdens to bear but somebody else's. You may call me an old fogy, but I would rather live cheap and dress plain than shirk my burdens because I had wasted when they had saved. You and John Hanson are both young and have got your health and strength, and instead of buying sealskins, and velvets and furbelows, you had better be laying up for a rainy day. You have no more need for a sealskin cloak than a cat has for a catechism. Now you do as you please, I have had my say."

Chapter XI

It has been quite a length of time since we left Mr. Thomas and his young friend facing an uncertain future. Since then he has not only been successful in building up a good business for himself, but in opening the gates to others. His success has not inflated him with pride. Neither has he become self-abashed and isolated from others less fortunate, who need his counsel and sympathy. Generous and noble in his character, he was conservative enough to cling to the good of the past and radical enough to give hospitality to every new idea which was calculated to benefit and make life noble and better. Mr. Thomas, in laying the foundation of his education, was thoughtful enough to enter a manual labor school, where he had the double advantage of getting an education and learning a trade, through which he was enabled to rely on himself without asking aid from any one, which in itself was an education in manliness, self-respect and self-reliance, that he could not have obtained had he been the protege of the wealthiest philanthropist in the land. As he had fine mechanical skill and ingenuity, he became an excellent carpenter. But it is one thing to have a trade and another thing to have an opportunity to exercise that trade. It was a time when a number of colored churches were being erected. To build large and even magnificent churches seemed to be a ruling passion with the colored people. Their homes might be very humble, their walls bare of pictured grace, but by united efforts they could erect large and handsome churches in which they had a common possession and it was one of the grand satisfactions of freedom that they were enabled to build their own churches and carry on their own business without being interfered with, and overlooked by a class of white ecclesiastics whose presence was a reminder of their implied inferiority. The church of which Mr. Thomas was a member was about to erect a costly edifice. The trustees would probably have willingly put the work in the hands of a colored man, had there been a sufficient number to have done the work, but they did not seem to remember that white prejudice had barred the Northern workshops against the colored man, that slavery, by degrading and monopolizing labor had been the means of educating colored men in the South to be good mechanics, and that a little pains and search on their part might have brought to light colored carpenters in the South who would have done the work as efficiently as those whom they employed, but as the trustees were not very farsighted men, they did the most available thing that came to hand; they employed a white man. Mr. Thomas' pastor applied to the master builder for a place for his parishioner.

"Can you give employment to one of my members, on our church?" Rev. Mr. Lomax asked the master builder.

"I would willingly do so, but I can not."

"Why not?"

"Because my men would all rise up against it. Now, for my part, I have no prejudice against your parishioner, but my men will not work with a colored man. I would let them all go if I could get enough colored men to suit me just as well, but such is the condition of the labor market, that a man must either submit to a number of unpalatable things or run the risk of a strike and being boycotted. I think some of these men who want so much liberty for themselves have very little idea of it for other people."

After this conversation the minister told Mr. Thomas the result of his interview with the master builder, and said,

"I am very sorry; but it is as it is, and it can't be any better."

"Do you mean by that that things are always going to remain as they are?"

"I do not see any quick way out of it. This prejudice is the outgrowth of ages; it did not come in a day, nor do I expect that it will vanish in an hour."

"Nor do I; but I do not think the best way for a people to mend their pastures is to sit down and bewail their fate."

"No; we must be up and going for ourselves. White people will——"

"White people," exclaimed Mr. Thomas somewhat impatiently. "Is there not a great deal of bosh in the estimate some of us have formed of white people. We share a common human feeling, from which the same cause produces the same effect. Why am I today a social Pariah, begging for work, and refused situation after situation? My father is a wealthy Southerner; he has several other sons who are inheritors of his name and heirs of his wealth. They are educated, cultured and occupy high social positions. Had I not as good a right to be well born as any of them? And yet, through my father's crime, I was doomed to the status of a slave with its heritage of ignorance, poverty and social debasement. Talk of the heathenism of Africa, of hostile tribes warring upon each other and selling the conquered foes into the hands of white men, but how much higher in the scale of moral progression was the white man who doomed his own child, bone of his bone, and flesh of his flesh, to a life of slavery? The heathen could plead in his defence the fortunes of war, and the hostility of an opposing tribe, but the white man who enslaved his child warred upon his hapless offspring and wrote chattel upon his condition when his hand was too feeble to hurl aside the accursed hand and recognize no other ownership but God. I once felt bitterly on this subject, and although it is impossible for my father to make full reparation for the personal wrong inflicted on me, I owe him no grudge. Hating is poor employment for any rational being, but I am not prepared to glorify him at the expense of my mother's race. She was faithful to me when he deserted me to a life of ignorance and poverty, and although three-fourths of the blood in my veins belongs to my father's face, I feel a kinship with my mother's people that I do not with his, and I will defend that race from the aspersions of the meanest Negro hater in the land. Heathenism and civilization live side by side on American soil, but all the heathenism is not on the side of the Negro. Look at slavery and kukluxism with their meanness and crimes, mormonism with its vile abominations, lynch law with its burnings and hangings, our national policy in regard to the Indians and Chinese."

"I do not think," said the minister, "that there is another civilized country in the world where men are lynched for real or supposed crimes outside of America."

"The Negro need not bow his head like a bulrush in the presence of a race whose records are as stained by crime and dishonor as theirs. Let others decry the Negro, and say hard things about him, I am not prepared to join in the chorus of depreciation."

After parting with the minister, Mr. Thomas resolved, if pluck and energy were of any avail, that he would leave no stone unturned in seeking employment. He searched the papers carefully for advertisements, walked from one workshop to the other looking for work, and was eventually met with a refusal which meant, no negro need apply. At last one day when he had tried almost every workshop in the place, he entered the establishment of Wm. C. Nell, an Englishman who had not been long enough in America to be fully saturated by its Christless and inhuman prejudices. He was willing to give Mr. Thomas work, and put tools in his hands, and while watching how deftly he handled them, he did not notice the indignant scowls on the faces of his workmen, and their murmurs of disapprobation as they uttered their dissatisfaction one to the other. At length they took off their aprons, laid down their tools and asked to be discharged from work.

"Why, what does this mean?" asked the astounded Englishman.

"It means that we will not work with a nigger."

"Why, I don't understand? what is the matter with him?"

"Why, there's nothing the matter, only he's a nigger, and we never put niggers on an equality with us, and we never will."

"But I am a stranger in this country, and I don't understand you."

"Well, he's a nigger, and we don't want niggers for nothing; would you have your daughter marry a nigger?"

"Oh, go back to your work; I never thought of such a thing. I think the Negro must be an unfortunate man, and I do not wish my daughter to marry any unfortunate man, but if you do not want to work with him I will put him by himself; there is room enough on the premises; will that suit you any better?"

"No; we won't work for a man who employs a nigger."

The builder bit his lip; he had come to America hearing that it was a land of liberty but he had found an undreamed of tyranny which had entered his workshop and controlled his choice of workmen, and as much as he deprecated the injustice, it was the dictum of a vitiated public opinion that his field of occupation should be closed against the Negro, and he felt that he was forced, either to give up his business or submit to the decree.

Mr. Thomas then thought, "my money is vanishing, school rooms and workshops are closed against me. I will not beg, and I can not resort to any questionable means for bread. I will now take any position or do any work by which I can make an honest living." Just as he was looking gloomily at the future an old school mate laid his hand upon his shoulder and said, "how do you do, old fellow? I have not seen you for a week of Sundays. What are you driving at now?"

"Oh, nothing in particular. I am looking for work."

"Well, now this is just the ticket. I have just returned from the Pacific coast and while I was there I did splendidly; everything I touched turned to gold, and now I have a good job on hand if you are not too squeamish to take it. I have just set up a tiptop restaurant and saloon, and I have some of the best merchants of the city as my customers, and I want a first rate clerk. You were always good at figures and if you will accept the place come with me right away. Since high license went into operation, I am making money hand over fist. It is just like the big fish eating up the little fish. I am doing a rushing business and I want you to do my clerking."

The first thought which rushed into Mr. Thomas' mind was, "Is thy servant a dog that he should do this thing?" but he restrained his indignation and said,

"No, Frank, I cannot accept your offer; I am a temperance man and a prohibitionist, and I would rather have my hands clean than to have them foul."

"You are a greater milksop than I gave you credit for. Here you are hunting work, and find door after door closed against you, not because you are not but because you are colored, and here am I offering you easy employment and good wages and you refuse them."

"Frank," said Mr. Thomas, "I am a poor man, but I would rather rise up early, and sit up late and eat the bread of carelessness, than to roll in wealth by keeping a liquor saloon, and I am determined that no drunkard shall ever charge me with having helped drag him down to misery, shame and death. No drunkard's wife shall ever lay the wreck of her home at my door."

"My business," said Frank Miller, "is a legitimate one; there is money in it, and I am after that. If people will drink too much and make fools of themselves I can't help it; it is none of my business, and if I don't sell to them other people will. I don't think much of a man who does not know how to govern himself, but it is no use arguing with you when you are once set in your ways; good morning."

Chapter XII

It was a gala day in Tennis Court. Annette had passed a highly successful examination, and was to graduate from the normal school, and as a matter of course, her neighbors wanted to hear Annette "speak her piece" as they called the commencement theme, and also to see how she was going to behave before all "them people." They were, generally speaking, too unaspiring to feel envious toward any one of their race who excelled them intellectually, and so there was little or no jealousy of Annette in Tennis Court; in fact some of her neighbors felt a kind of pride in the thought that Tennis Court would turn out a girl who could stand on the same platform and graduate alongside of some of their employers' daughters. If they could not stand there themselves they were proud that one of their race could.

"I feel," said one, "like the boy when some one threatened to slap off his face who said 'you can slap off my face, but I have a big brother and you can't slap off his face;'" and strange as it may appear, Annette received more encouragement from a class of honest-hearted but ignorant and well meaning people who knew her, than she did from some of the most cultured and intelligent people of A.P. Nor was it very strange; they were living too near the poverty, ignorance and social debasement of the past to have developed much race pride, and a glowing enthusiasm in its progress and development. Although they were of African descent, they were Americans whose thoughts were too much Americanized to be wholly free from imbibing the social atmosphere with which they were in constant contact in their sphere of enjoyments. The literature they read was mostly from the hands of white men who would paint them in any colors which suited their prejudices or predilections. The religious ideas they had embraced came at first thought from the same sources, though they may have undergone modifications in passing through their channels of thought, and it must be a remarkable man or woman who thinks an age ahead of the generation in which his or her lot is cast, and who plans and works for the future on the basis of that clearer vision. Nor is it to be wondered at, if under the circumstances, some of the more cultured of A.P. thought it absurd to look for anything remarkable to come out of the black Nazareth of Tennis court. Her neighbors had an idea that Annette was very smart; that she had a great "head piece," but unless she left A.P. to teach school elsewhere, they did not see what good her education was going to do her. It wasn't going to put any meal in the barrel nor any potatoes in the bin. Even Mrs. Larkins relaxed her ancient hostility to Annette and opened her heart to present her with a basket of flowers. Annette within the last year had become very much changed in her conduct and character. She had become friendly in her manner and considerate in her behavior to Mrs. Larkins since she had entered the church, during a protracted meeting. Annette was rather crude in her religious views but here again Mrs. Lasette became her faithful friend and advisor. In dealing with a young convert she thought more was needed than getting her into the church and making her feel that the moment she rose from the altar with rejoicing on her lips, that she was a full blown christian. That, to Mrs. Lasette was the initial step in the narrow way left luminous by the bleeding feet of Christ, and what the young convert needed was to be taught how to walk worthy of her high calling, and to make her life a thing of usefulness and faithfulness to God and man, a growth in grace and in the saving knowledge of our Lord Jesus Christ. Simply attired in a dress which Mrs. Lasette thought fitted for the occasion, Annette took her seat quietly on the platform and calmly waited till her turn came. Her subject was announced: "The Mission of the Negro." It was a remarkable production for a girl of her age. At first she portrayed an African family seated beneath their bamboo huts and spreading palms; the light steps of the young men and maidens tripping to music, dance and song; their pastimes suddenly broken upon by the tramp of the merchants of flesh and blood; the capture of defenceless people suddenly surprised in the midst of their sports, the cries of distress, the crackling of flames, the cruel oaths of reckless men, eager for gold though they coined it from tears and extracted it from blood; the crowding of the slaveships, the horrors of the middle passage, the landing of the ill-fated captives were vividly related, and the sad story of ages of bondage. It seemed as if the sorrow of centuries was sobbing in her voice. Then the scene changed, and like a grand triumphal march she recounted the deliverance of the Negro, and the wondrous change which had come over his condition; the slave pen exchanged for the free school, the fetters on his wrist for the ballot in his right hand. Then her voice grew musical when she began to speak of the mission of the Negro, "His mission," she said, "is grandly constructive." Some races had been "architects of destruction," but their mission was to build over the ruins of the dead past, the most valuable thing that a man or woman could possess on earth, and that is good character. That mission should be to bless and not to curse. To lift up the banner of the Christian religion from the mire and dust into which slavery and pride of caste had trailed it, and to hold it up as an ensign of hope and deliverance to other races of the world, of whom the greater portion were not white people. It seemed as if an inspiration lit up the young face; her eye glowed with unwonted fervor; it seemed as if she had fused her whole soul into the subject, which was full of earnestness and enthusiasm. Her theme was the sensation of the hour. Men grew thoughtful and attentive, women tender and sympathetic as they heard this member of a once despised people, recount the trials and triumphs of her race, and the hopes that gathered around their future. The day before Annette graduated Mr. Thomas had met a friend of his at Mrs. Lasette's, who had lately returned from an extensive tour. He had mingled with many people and had acquired a large store of information. Mr. Thomas had invited him to accompany him to the commencement. He had expected that Annette would acquit herself creditably, but she had far exceeded his most sanguine expectations. Clarence Luzerne had come because his friend Mr. Thomas had invited him and because he and Mrs. Lasette had taken such great interest in Annette's welfare, and his curiosity was excited to see how she would acquit herself and compare with the other graduates. He did not have much faith in graduating essays. He had heard a number of such compositions at commencements which had inspired him with glowing hopes for the future of the authors, which he had never seen realized, and he had come more to gratify Mr. Thomas than to please himself. But if he came through curiosity, he remained through interest, which had become more and more absorbing as she proceeded.

"Clarence," said Mr. Thomas to his friend, noticing the deep interest he was manifesting, "Are you entranced? You appear perfectly spell-bound."

"Well, I am; I am really delighted and indebted to you for a rare and unexpected pleasure. Why, that young lady gave the finest production that I have heard this morning. I hardly think she could have written it herself. It seems wonderful that a girl of her age should have done it so well. You are a great friend of hers; now own up, are not your finger marks upon it? I wouldn't tell it out of our ranks, but I don't think she wrote that all herself."

"Who do you think wrote it for her?"

"Mrs. Lasette."

"I do not think so; Mrs. Lasette is a fine writer, but that nervous, fervid and impassioned style is so unlike hers, that I do not think she wrote one line of it, though she might have overlooked it, and made some suggestions, but even if it were so that some one else wrote it, we know that no one else delivered it, and that her delivery was excellent."

"That is so; why, she excelled all the other girls. Do you know what was the difference between her and the other girls?"

"No; what was it?" said Mr. Thomas.

"They wrote from their heads, she wrote from her heart. Annette has begun to think; she has been left a great deal to herself, and in her loneliness, she has developed a thoughtfulness past her years, and I think that a love for her race and a desire to serve it has become a growing passion in her soul; her heart has supplied her intellect."

"Ah, I think from what you say that I get the true clue to the power and pathos with which she spoke this morning and that accounts for her wonderful success."

"Yes," said Mr. Luzerne,[14] "it is the inner life which develops the outer life, and just such young people as Annette make me more hopeful of the future of the race."

Mrs. Lasette witnessed Annette's graduation with intense interest and pleasure. Grandmother Harcourt looked the very impersonation of satisfaction as she gathered up the floral gifts, and modestly waited while Annette received the pleasant compliments of admiring friends.

At his request Mr. Thomas introduced Mr. Luzerne to Annette, who in the most gracious and affable manner, tendered to Annette his hearty congratulations which she modestly received, and for the time being all went merry as a marriage bell.

Chapter XIII

"What a fool he is to refuse my offer," thought the saloon-keeper. "What a pity it is," said Mr. Thomas to himself, "that a man of his education and ability should be engaged in such accursed business."

After refusing the saloonkeeper's offer Mr. Thomas found a job of work. It was not a job congenial to his feelings, but his motto was, "If I do not see an opening I will make one." After he had turned from Mr. Englishman's workshop, burning with a sense of wrong which he felt powerless to overcome, he went on the levee and looked around to see if any work might be picked up by him as a day laborer. He saw a number of men singing, joking and plying their tasks with nimble feet and apparently no other care upon their minds than meeting the demands of the present hour, and for a moment he almost envied their lightheartedness, and he thought within himself, where all men are born blind, no man misses the light. These men are contented with privileges, and I who have fitted myself for a different sphere in life, am chaffing because I am denied rights. The right to sell my labor in any workshop in this city same as the men of other nationalities, and to receive with them a fair day's wages for a fair day's work. But he was strong and healthy and he was too high spirited to sit moping at home depending upon his mother to divide with him her scanty means till something should turn up. The first thing that presented itself to him was the job of helping unload a boat which had landed at the wharf, and a hand was needed to assist in unloading her. Mr. Thomas accepted the position and went to work and labored manfully at the unaccustomed task. That being finished the merchant for whom he had done the work, hired him to labor in his warehouse. He showed himself very handy in making slight repairs when needed and being ready to turn his hand to any service out of his routine of work, hammering a nail, adjusting a disordered lock and showing a general concern in his employer's interests. One day his employer had engaged a carpenter to make him a counter, but the man instead of attending to his work had been off on a drunken spree, and neglected to do the job. The merchant, vexed at the unnecessary delay, said to Mr. Thomas in a bantering manner, "I believe you can do almost anything, couldn't you make this counter?"

Mr. Thomas answered quite modestly, "I believe I could if I had my tools."

"Tools! What do you mean by tools?"

Mr. Thomas told him how he learned to be a carpenter in the South and how he had tried so unsuccessfully in the North to get an opportunity to work at his trade until discouraged with the attempt, he had made up his mind to take whatever work came to hand till he could see farther.

The merchant immediately procured the materials and set Mr. Thomas to work, who in a short time finished the counter, and showed by his workmanship that he was an excellent carpenter. The merchant pleased with his work and satisfied with his ability, entrusted him with the erection of a warehouse and, strange as it may appear, some of those men who were too proud or foolish to work with him as a fellow laborer, were humble enough to work under him as journeymen. When he was down they were ready to kick him down. When he was up they were ready to receive his helping hand. Mr. Thomas soon reached that "tide in his affairs which taken at the flood leads on to fortune." Against the odds which were against him his pluck and perseverance prevailed, and he was enabled not only to build up a good business for himself, but also to help others, and to teach them by his own experience not to be too easily discouraged, but to trust to pluck more than luck, and learn in whatever capacity they were employed to do their work heartily as unto the Lord and not unto men.

Anxious to do what she could to benefit the community in which she lived, Mrs. Lasette threw open her parlors for the gathering together of the best thinkers and workers of the race, who choose to avail themselves of the privilege of meeting to discuss any question of vital importance to the welfare of the colored people of the nation. Knowing the entail of ignorance which slavery had left them, she could not be content by shutting up herself to mere social enjoyments within the shadow of her home. And often the words would seem to ring within her soul, "my people is destroyed for lack of knowledge," and with those words would come the question, am I doing what I can to dispel the darkness which has hung for centuries around our path? I have been blessed with privileges which were denied others; I sat 'mid the light of knowledge when some of my ill-fated sisters did not know what it was to see daylight in their cabins from one week's end to the other. Sometimes when she met with coldness and indifference where she least expected it, she would grow sad but would not yield to discouragement. Her heart was in the right place. "Freely she had received and freely she would give." It was at one of Mrs. Lasette's gatherings that Mr. Thomas met Rev. Mr. Lomax on whose church he had been refused a place, and Mr. Thurman, a tradesman who also had been ousted from his position through pride of caste and who had gone into another avocation, and also Charley Cooper, of whom we have lost sight for a number of years. He is now a steady and prosperous young man, a constant visitor at Mrs. Lasette's. Rumor says that Mrs. Lasette's bright-eyed and lovely daughter is the magnet which attracts him to their pleasant home. Rev. Lomax has also been absent for several years on other charges, but when he meets Mr. Thomas, the past flows back and the incidents of their latest interviews naturally take their place in the conversation. "It has been some time since we met," said Mr. Thomas, heartily shaking the minister's hand.

"How has life used you since last we met?" said Rev. Lomax to Mr. Thomas. "Are you well?"

"Perfectly well, I have had a varied experience since I met you, but I have no reason to complain, and I think my experience has been invaluable to me, and with this larger experience and closer observation, I feel that I am more able to help others, and that, I feel, has been one of my most valued acquirements. I sometimes think of members of our people in some directions as sheep without a shepherd, and I do wish from the bottom of my heart that I knew the best way to help them."

"You do not," said the minister, somewhat anxiously, "ignore the power of the pulpit."

"No, I do not; I only wish it had tenfold force. I wish we had ten thousand ministers like Oberlin who was not ashamed to take the lead in opening a road from Bande Roche to Strasburgh, a distance of several miles to bring his parishioners in contact with the trade and business of a neighboring village. I hope the time will come when every minister in building a church which he consecrates to the worship of God will build alongside of it or under the same roof, parish buildings or rooms to be dedicated to the special wants of our people in their peculiar condition."

"I do wish, Brother Lomax, those costly buildings which you erect will cover more needs and wants of our people than some of them do now."

"What would you have in them?"

"I would have a parish building to every church, and I would have in them an evening home for boys. I would have some persons come in and teach them different handicrafts, so as at least to give them an opportunity to be more expert in learning how to use their hands. I would have that building a well warmed and well lighted room in winter, where all should be welcome to come and get a sandwich and a warm cup of tea or coffee and a hot bowl of soup, and if the grogshops were selling liquor for five cents, I would sell the soup for three or four cents, with a roll. I would have a room reserved for such ladies as Mrs. Lasette, who are so willing to help, for the purpose of holding mother's meetings. I would try to have the church the great centre of moral, spiritual and intellectual life for the young, and try to present counter attractions to the debasing influence of the low grogshops, gambling dens and houses of ill fame."

"Part of our city (ought I confine myself to saying part of the city) has not the whole city been cursed by rum? But I now refer to a special part. I have seen church after church move out of that part of the city where the nuisance and curse were so rife, but I never, to my knowledge, heard of one of those churches offering to build a reading room and evening home for boys, or to send out paid and sustained by their efforts, a single woman to go into rum-cursed homes and teach their inmates a more excellent way. I would have in that parish building the most earnest men and women to come together and consult and counsel with each other on the best means to open for ourselves, doors which are still closed against us."

"I am sure," said the minister, "I am willing to do what I can for the temporal and spiritual welfare of our people, and in this I have the example of the great Physician who did not consider it beneath him to attend to physical maladies as well as spiritual needs, and who did not consider the synagogue too holy, nor the Sabbath day too sacred to administer to the destitute and suffering."

"I was very sorry when I found out, Brother Thomas, that I could not have you employed on my church, but I do not see what else I could have done except submit."

"That was all you could have done in that stage of the work when I applied, and I do not wish to bestow the slightest censure on you or the trustees of your church, but I think, if when you were about to build had you advertised for competent master-builders in the South, that you could have gotten enough to have built the church without having employed Mr. Hoog the master-builder. Had you been able to have gone to him and said, 'we are about to build a church and it is more convenient for us to have it done by our citizens than to send abroad for laborers. We are in communication with a colored master builder in Kentucky, who is known as an efficient workman and who would be glad to get the job, and if your men refuse to work with a colored man our only alternative will be to send for colored carpenters and put the building in their hands.' Do you think he would have refused a thirty thousand dollar job just because some of his men refused to work with colored men? I think the greater portion of his workmen would have held their prejudices in abeyance rather than let a thirty thousand dollar job slip out of their hands. Now here is another thing in which I think united effort could have effected something. Now, here is my friend Mr. Thurman; he was a saddler versed in both branches of harness making. For awhile he got steady work in a saddler's shop, but the prejudice against him was so great that his employer was forced to dismiss him. He took work home, but that did not heal the dissatisfaction, and at last he gave it up and went to well-digging. Now, there were colored men in that place who could have, as I think, invested some money in buying material and helped him, not as a charity, but as a mere business operation to set up a place for himself; he had the skill; they had the money, and had they united both perhaps to-day there would be a flourishing business carried on by the man who is now digging wells for a living. I do hope that some time there will be some better modes of communication between us than we now possess; that a labor bureau will be established not as a charity among us, but as a business with capable and efficient men who will try to find out the different industries that will employ men irrespective of color and advertise and find steady and reliable colored men to fill them. Colored men in the South are largely employed in raising cotton and other produce; why should there not be more openings in the South for colored men to handle the merchandize and profit by it?"

"What hinders?" said Rev. Lomax.

"I will not say what hinders, but I will say what I think you can try to do to help. Teach our young to dedicate their young lives to the noble service of devoting them to the service of our common cause; to throw away their cigars, dash down the foaming beer and sparkling wine and strive to be more like those of whom it was said, 'I write unto you, young men, because you are strong.'"

Chapter XIV

Grandmother Harcourt was failing. Annette was rising towards life's summit. Her grandmother was sinking to death's vale.

> The hours are rifting day by day
> Strength from the walls of living clay.

Her two children who were living in A.P. wished her to break up her home and come and live with them. They had room in their hearts and homes for her, but not for Annette. There was something in Annette's temperament with which other members of the family could not harmonize. They were not considerate enough to take into account her antenatal history, and to pity where they were so ready to condemn. Had Annette been born deficient in any of her bodily organs, they could have made allowance for her, and would have deemed it cruel to have demanded that she should have performed the same amount of labor with one hand that she could have done with both. They knew nothing of heredity, except its effects, which they were not thoughtful enough to trace back to the causes over which Annette had no control, and instead of trying to counteract them as one might strive to do in a case of inherited physical tendencies, they only aggravated, and constantly strengthened all the unlovely features in Annette's character, and Annette really seemed like an anomalous contradiction. There was a duality about her nature as if the blood of two races were mingling in her veins. To some persons Annette was loving and love-able, bright, intelligent, obliging and companionable; to others, unsociable, unamiable and repelling. Her heart was like a harp which sent out its harmonious discords in accordance with the moods of the player who touched its chords. To some who swept them it gave out tender and touching melody, to others its harshest and saddest discords. Did not the Psalmist look beneath the mechanism of the body to the constitution of the soul when he said that "We are fearfully and wonderfully made?"

But the hour came when all discussion was ended as to who was to shelter the dear old grandmother in her declining years. Mrs. Harcourt was suddenly paralyzed, and in a few days Annette stood doubly orphaned. Grandmother Harcourt's children gathered around the bedside of their dying mother. She was conscious but unable to speak. Occasionally her eyes would rest lovingly upon Annette and then turn wistfully to her children. Several times she assayed to speak, but the words died upon her lips. Her eldest son entered the room just as life was trembling on its faintest chords. She recognized him, and gathering up her remaining strength she placed his hand on Annette's, and tried again to speak. He understood her and said very tenderly,

"Mother, I will look after Annette."

All the care faded from the dear old face. Amid the shadows that never deceive flitted a smile of peace and contentment. The fading eye lit up with a sudden gaze of joy and wonder. She reached out her hand as if to meet a welcome and precious friend, and then the radiant face grew deathly pale; the outstretched hands relaxed their position, and with a smile, just such a smile as might greet a welcoming angel, her spirit passed out into the eternities, and Annette felt as she had never felt before, that she was all alone. The love that had surrounded and watched over her, born with her perverseness, and sheltered her in its warm clasp, was gone; it had faded suddenly from her vision, and left in its stead a dull and heavy pain. After the funeral, Mrs. Harcourt's children returned to the house where they quietly but earnestly discussed the question what shall be done with Annette. Mrs. Hanson's house was rather small; that is, it was rather small for Annette. She would have found room in her house if she only had room in her heart for her. She had nursed her mother through her sickness, and said with unnatural coldness, "I have got rid of one trouble and I do not want another." Another sister who lived some distance from A.P., would have taken Annette, but she knew that other members of her family would object, as they would be fearful that Annette would be an apple of discord among them. At length, her uncle Thomas decided that she should go with him. He felt that his mother had died with the assurance on her mind that he would care for Annette, and he resolved to be faithful in accepting what was to him the imposition of a new burden on his shoulders. His wife was a cold and unsympathizing woman. She was comfortably situated but did not wish that comfort invaded by her husband's relations. In household matters her husband generally deferred to her judgment, but here was no other alternative than that of taking Annette under the shadow of his home, or leaving her unprotected in the wide world, and he was too merciful and honorable to desert Annette in her saddest hour of need. Having determined that Annette should share his home, he knew that it was advisable to tell his wife about his decision, and to prepare her for Annette's coming.

"Well," said Dr. Harcourt's wife after her husband's return from the funeral, "what are you going to do with Annette?"

"She is coming here," said Dr. Harcourt quietly and firmly.

"Coming here?" said Mrs. Harcourt, looking aghast. "I think at least you might have consulted me."

"That is true, my dear, I would have gladly done so had you been present when the decision was made."

"But where are her aunts, and where was your brother, John; why didn't they take her?"

"John was at home sick with the rheumatism and sister Jane did not appear to be willing to have her come."

"I guess Jane is like I am; got enough to do to look after her own family."

"And sister Eliza said she hadn't any room."

"No room; when she has eight rooms in her house and only two children? She could have made room for her had she chosen."

"May be her husband wasn't willing."

"Oh, it is no such thing. I know John Hanson[15] better than that; Liza is the head man of that house, and just leads him by the nose wherever she wants him to go, and besides, Mrs. Lord's daughter is there pretending to pay board, but I don't believe that she pays it one-half the time."

"She is company for Alice and they all seem very fond of her."

"I do get so sick of that girl, mambying and jambying about that family; calling Liza and her husband 'Ma and Pa,' I haven't a bit of faith in her."

"Well, I confess that I am not very much preposessed in her favor. She just puts me in mind of a pussy cat purring around you."

"Well, now as to Annette. You do not want her here?"

"Not if I can help it."

"But can't she help you to work?"

"She could if she knew how. If wishes were horses beggars might ride. Your mother made a great mistake in bringing Annette up. Annette has a good education, but when that is said, all is said."

"Why, my dear mother was an excellent housekeeper. Did she not teach Annette?"

"Your mother was out a great deal as a sick nurse, and when she went away from home she generally boarded Annette with a friend, who did not, as your mother paid her good board, exact any service from Annette, and while with her she never learned to make a loaf of bread or to cook a beefsteak, and when your mother was at home when she set Annette to do any work, if she did it awkwardly and clumsily she would take it out of her hand and do it herself rather than bother with her, and now I suppose I am to have all the bother and worry with her."

"Well my dear."

"Oh don't come dearing me, and bringing me all this trouble."

"Well my dear, I don't see how it could be helped. I could not leave Annette in the house all by herself. I couldn't afford to make myself the town's talk. May be things will turn out better than you expect. We've got children of our own, and we don't know when we are gone, how they will fare."

"That is true, but I never mean to bring my children up in such a way that they will be no use anywhere, and no one will want them."

"Well, I don't see any other way than bringing Annette here."

"Well, if I must, I must," she said with an air of despondency.

Dr. Harcourt rode over to his sister's where Annette was spending the day and brought the doubly orphaned girl to his home. As she entered the room, it seemed as though a chill struck to her heart when her Aunt bade her good morning. There was no warm pressure in the extended hand. No loving light in the cold unsympathizing eyes which seemed to stab her through and through. The children eyed her inquisitively, as if wishing to understand her status with their parents before they became sociable with her. After supper Annette's uncle went out and her aunt sat quietly and sewed till bed time, and then showed Annette to her room and left the lonely girl to herself and her great sorrow. Annette sat silent, tearless, and alone. Grief had benumbed her faculties. She had sometimes said when grandmother had scolded her that "she was growing cross and cold." But oh, what would she not have given to have had the death-created silence broken by that dear departed voice, to have felt the touch of a vanished hand, to have seen again the loving glance of the death darkened eye. But it was all over; no tears dimmed her eye, as she sat thinking so mournfully of her great sorrow, till she unfastened from her neck a little keepsake containing a lock of grandmother's hair, then all the floodgates of her soul were opened and she threw herself upon her bed and sobbed herself to sleep. In the morning she awoke with that sense of loss and dull agony which only they know, who have seen the grave close over all they have held dearest on earth. The beautiful home of her uncle was very different from the humble apartments; here she missed all the freedom and sunshine that she had enjoyed beneath the shelter of her grandmother's roof.

"Can you sew?" said her aunt to Annette, as she laid on the table a package of handkerchiefs.

"Yes ma'm."

"Let me see how you can do this," handing her one to hem. Annette hemmed the handkerchief nicely; her aunt examined it, put it down and gave her some others to hem, but there was no word of encouragement for her, not even a pleasant, "well done." They both relapsed into silence; between them there was no pleasant interchange of thought. Annette was tolerated and endured, but she did not feel that she was loved and welcomed. It was no place to which she could invite her young friends to spend a pleasant evening. Once she invited some of her young friends to her home, but she soon found that it was a liberty which she should be careful never to repeat. Soon after Annette came to live with her aunt her aunt's mother had a social gathering and reunion of the members of her family. All Dr. Harcourt's children were invited, from the least to the greatest, but poor Annette was left behind. Mrs. Lasette, who happened in the house the evening before the entertainment, asked, "Is not Annette going?" when Mrs. Harcourt replied, very coldly, "She is not one of the family," referring to her mother's family circle.

A shadow flitted over the face of Mrs. Lasette; she thought of her own daughter and how sad it would be to have her live in such a chilly atmosphere of social repression and neglect at a period of life when there was so much danger that false friendship might spread their lures for her inexperienced feet. I will criticize, she said to herself, by creation. I, too, have some social influence, if not among the careless, wine-bibbing, ease-loving votaries of fashion, among some of the most substantial people of A.P., and as long as Annette preserves her rectitude at my house she shall be a welcome guest and into that saddened life I will bring all the sunshine that I can.

Chapter XV

"Well mama," said Mrs. Lasette's daughter to her mother, "I cannot understand why you take so much interest in Annette. She is very unpopular. Scarcely any of the girls ever go with her, and even her cousin never calls for her to go to church or anywhere else, and I sometimes feel so sorry to see her so much by herself, and some of the girls when I went with her to the exposition, said that they wouldn't have asked her to have gone with them, that she isn't our set."

"Poor child," Mrs. Lasette replied; "I am sorry for her. I hope that you will never treat her unkindly, and I do not think if you knew the sad story connected with her life that you would ever be unkind enough to add to the burden she has been forced to bear."

"But mamma, Annette is so touchy. Her aunt says that her tear bags must lay near her eyes and that she will cry if you look at her, and that she is the strangest, oddest creature she ever saw, and I heard she did not wish her to come."

"Why, my dear child, who has been gossipping to you about your neighbors?"

"Why, Julia Thomas."

"Well, my daughter, don't talk after her; gossip is liable to degenerate into evil speaking and then I think it tends to degrade and belittle the mind to dwell on the defects and imperfections of our neighbors. Learn to dwell on the things that are just and true and of good report, but I am sorry for Annette, poor child."

"What makes her so strange, do you know?"

"Yes," said Mrs. Lasette somewhat absently.

"If you do, won't you tell me?"

Again Mrs. Lasette answered in the same absent manner.

"Why mama, what is the matter with you; you say yes to everything and yet you are not paying any attention to anything that I say. You seem like someone who hears, but does not listen; who sees, but does not look. Your face reminds me of the time when I showed you the picture of a shipwreck and you said, 'My brother's boat went down in just such a fearful storm.'"

"My dear child," said Mrs. Lasette, rousing up from a mournful reverie, "I was thinking of a wreck sadder, far sadder than the picture you showed me. It was the mournful wreck of a blighted life."

"Whose life, mama?"

"The life of Annette's [grand]mother. We were girls together and I loved her dearly," Mrs. Lasette replied as tears gathered in her eyes when she recalled one of the saddest memories of her life.

"Do tell me all about it, for I am full of curiosity."

"My child, I want this story to be more than food for your curiosity; I want it to be a lesson and a warning to you. Annette's grandmother was left to struggle as breadwinner for a half dozen children when her husband died. Then there were not as many openings for colored girls as there are now. Our chief resource was the field of domestic service, and circumstances compelled Annette's mother to live out, as we called it. In those days we did not look down upon a girl and try to ostracize her from our social life if she was forced to be a servant. If she was poor and respectable we valued her for what she was rather than for what she possessed. Of course we girls liked to dress nicely, but fine clothes was not the chief passport to our society, and yet I think on the whole that our social life would compare favorably with yours in good character, if not in intellectual attainments. Our dear old mothers were generally ignorant of books, but they did try to teach good manners and good behavior; but I do not think they saw the danger around the paths of the inexperienced with the same clearness of vision we now do. Mrs. Harcourt had unbounded confidence in her children, and as my mother thought, gave her girls too much rein in their own hands. Our mother was more strict with her daughters and when we saw Mrs. Harcourt's daughters having what we considered such good times, I used to say, 'O, I wish mother wasn't so particular!' Other girls could go unattended to excursions, moonlight drives and parties of pleasure, but we never went to any such pleasure unless we were attended by our father, brother or some trusted friend of the family. We were young and foolish then and used to chafe against her restrictions; but to-day, when I think of my own good and noble husband, my little bright and happy home, and my dear, loving daughter, I look back with gratitude to her thoughtful care and honor and bless her memory in her grave. Poor Lucy Harcourt was not so favored; she was pretty and attractive and had quite a number of admirers. At length she became deeply interested in a young man who came as a stranger to our city. He was a fine looking man, but there was something about him from which I instinctively shrank. My mother felt the same way and warned us to be careful how we accepted any attention from him; but poor Lucy became perfectly infatuated with him and it was rumored that they were to be shortly married. Soon after the rumor he left the city and there was a big change in Lucy's manner. I could not tell what was the matter, but my mother forbade me associating with her, and for several months I scarcely saw her, but I could hear from others that she was sadly changed. Instead of being one of the most light-hearted girls, I heard that she used to sit day after day in her mother's house and wring her hands and weep and that her mother's heart was almost broken. Friends feared that Lucy was losing her mind and might do some desperate deed, but she did not. I left about that time to teach school in a distant village, and when I returned home I heard sad tidings of poor Lucy. She was a mother, but not a wife. Her brothers had grown angry with her for tarnishing their family name, of which they were so proud; her mother's head was bowed with agony and shame. The father of Lucy's child had deserted her in her hour of trial and left her to bear her burden alone with the child like a millstone around her neck. Poor Lucy; I seldom saw her after that, but one day I met her in the Park. I went up to her and kissed her, she threw her arms around me and burst into a flood of tears. I tried to restrain her from giving such vent to her feelings. It was a lack of self-control which had placed her where she was."

"'Oh Anna!' she said, 'it does me so much good to hold your hand in mine once more. I reminds me of the days when we used to be together. Oh, what would I give to recall those days.'"

"I said to her, Lucy, you can never recall the past, but you can try to redeem the future. Try to be a faithful mother. Men may build over the wreck and ruin of their young lives a better and brighter future, why should not a woman? Let the dead past bury its dead and live in the future for the sake of your child. She seemed so grateful for what I had said. Others had treated her with scorn. Her brother Thomas had refused to speak to her; her betrayer had forsaken her; all the joyousness had faded from her life and, poor girl, I was glad that I was able to say a helpful and hopeful word to her. Mother, of course, would not let us associate with her, but she always treated her kindly when she came and did what she could to lighten the burden which was pressing her down to the grave. But, poor child, she was never again the same light-hearted girl. She grew pale and thin and in the hectic flush and faltering tread I read the death sign of early decay, and I felt that my misguided young friend was slowly dying of a broken heart. Then there came a day when we were summoned to her dying bed. Her brothers and sisters were present; all their resentment against her had vanished in the presence of death. She was their dear sister about to leave them and they bent in tearful sorrow around her couch. As one of her brothers, who was a good singer, entered the room, she asked him to sing 'Vital spark of heavenly flame.' He attempted to sing, but there were tremors in his voice and he faltered in the midst of the hymn. 'Won't you sing for your dying sister.'"

"Again he essayed to sing, but [his?] voice became choked with emotion, and he ceased, and burst into tears. Her brother Thomas who had been so hard and cold, and had refused to speak to her, now wept and sobbed like a child, but Lucy smiled as she bade them good bye, and exclaimed, 'Welcome death, the end of fear. I am prepared to die.' A sweet peace settled down on her face, and Lucy had exchanged, I hope, the sorrow and pain of life for the peace and rest of heaven, and left Annette too young to know her loss. Do you wonder then my child that I feel such an interest in Annette and that knowing as I do her antenatal history that I am ever ready to pity where others condemn, and that I want to do what I can to help round out in beauty and usefulness the character of that sinned against and disinherited child, whose restlessness and sensitiveness I trace back to causes over which she had no control."

"What became of Frank Miller? You say that when he returned to A.P. that society opened its doors to him while they were closed to Annette's mother. I don't understand it. Was he not as guilty as she was?"

"Guiltier, I think. If poor Lucy failed as a woman, she tried to be faithful as a mother, while he, faithless as a man, left her to bear her burden alone. She was frail as a woman, but he was base, mean, and selfish as a man."

"How was it that society received him so readily?"

"All did not receive him so readily, but with some his money, like charity, covered a multitude of sins. But from the depths of my heart I despised him. I had not then learned to hate the sin with all my heart, and yet the sinner love. To me he was the incarnation of social meanness and vice. And just as I felt I acted. We young folks had met at a social gathering, and were engaged in a pastime in which we occasionally clasped hands together. Some of these plays I heartily disliked, especially when there was romping and promiscuous kissing. During the play Frank Miller's hand came in contact with mine and he pressed it. I can hardly describe my feelings. It seemed as if my very veins were on fire, and that every nerve was thrilling with repulsion and indignation. Had I seen him murder Lucy and then turn with blood dripping hands to grasp mine, I do not think that I should have felt more loathing than I did when his hand clasped mine. I felt that his very touch was pollution; I immediately left the play, tore off my glove, and threw it in the fire."

"Oh, mother, how could you have done so? You are so good and gentle."

Mrs. Lasette replied, "I was not always so. I do not hate his sin any less now than I did then but I think that I have learned a Christian charity which would induce me to pluck such as he out of the fire while I hated the garments spotted by his sins. I sat down trembling with emotion. I heard a murmur of disapprobation. There was a check to the gayety of the evening. Frank Miller, bold and bad as he was looked crestfallen and uneasy. Some who appeared to be more careful of the manners of society than its morals, said that I was very rude. Others said that I was too prudish, and would be an old maid, that I was looking for perfection in young men, and would not find it. That young men sow their wild oats, and that I was more nice than wise, and that I would frighten the gentlemen away from me. I told them if the young men were so easily frightened, that I did not wish to clasp hands for life with any such timid set, and that I was determined that I would have a moral husband or none; that I was not obliged to be married, but that I was obliged to be true to my conscience. That when I married I expected to lay the foundation of a new home, and that I would never trust my future happiness in the hands of a libertine, or lay its foundations over the reeling brain of a drunkard, and I determined that I would never marry a man for whose vices I must blush, and whose crimes I must condone; that while I might bend to grief I would not bow to shame; that if I brought him character and virtue, he should give me true manhood and honor in return."

"And I think mother that you got it when you married father."

"I am satisfied that I did, and the respect and appreciation my daughter has for her father is only part of my life's reward, but it was my dear mother who taught me to distinguish between the true and the false, and although she was [not?] what you call educated, she taught me that no magnificence of fortune would atone for meanness of spirit, that without character the most wealthy and talented man is a bankrupt in soul. And she taught me how to be worthy of a true man's love."

"And I think you have succeeded splendidly."

"Thank you, my darling. But mother has become used to compliments."

Chapter XVI

"I do not think she gets any more than she deserves," said Mr. Lasette, entering the room. "She is one of whom it may be said, 'Her children arise up and call her blessed, her husband also, and he praiseth her; many daughters have done virtuously but thou excellest them all.'"

"I do not think you will say that I am excelling if I do not haste about your supper; you were not home to dinner and must be hungry by this time, and it has been said that the way to a man's heart is through his stomach."

"Oh, isn't that a libel on my sex!"

"Papa," said Laura Lasette, after her mother had left the room, "did you know Frank Miller? Mother was telling me about him but she did not finish; what became of him?"

"Now, you ask me two questions in one breath; let me answer one at a time."

"Well, papa, I am all attention."

"Do I know Frank Miller, the saloon keeper? Yes; he is connected with a turning point in my life. How so? Well, just be patient a minute and I will tell you. I was almost a stranger in A.P. when I first met your mother. It was at a social where Frank Miller was a guest. I had heard some very damaging reports concerning his reputation, but from the manner in which he was received in society, I concluded that I had been misinformed. Surely, I thought, if the man is as vicious as he has been represented, good women, while they pity him, will shrink instinctively from him, but I saw to my surprise, that with a confident and unblushing manner, he moved among what was called the elite of the place, and that instead of being withheld, attentions were lavished upon him. I had lived most of my life in a small inland town, where people were old fashioned enough to believe in honor and upright conduct, and from what I had heard of Frank Miller I was led to despise his vices and detest his character, and yet here were women whom I believed to be good and virtuous, smiling in his face, and graciously receiving his attentions. I cannot help thinking that in their case,

"Evil is wrought by want of thought"
As well as want of heart.

They were not conscious of the influence they might exert by being true to their own womanhood. Men like Frank Miller are the deadliest foes of women. One of the best and strongest safe guards of the home is the integrity of its women, and he who undermines that, strikes a fearful blow at the highest and best interests of society. Society is woman's realm and I never could understand how, if a woman really loves purity for its own worth and loveliness, she can socially tolerate men whose lives are a shame, and whose conduct in society is a blasting, withering curse."

"But, papa, tell me how you came to love my mother; but I don't see how you could have helped it."

"That's just it, my daughter. I loved her because I could not help it; and respected her because I knew that she was worthy of respect. I was present at a social gathering where Frank was a guest, and was watching your mother attentively when I saw her shrink instinctively from his touch and leave the play in which she was engaged and throw her glove in the fire. Public opinion was divided about her conduct. Some censured, others commended her, but from that hour I learned to love her, and I became her defender. Other women would tolerate Frank Miller, but here was a young and gracious girl, strong enough and brave enough to pour on the head of that guilty culprit her social disapprobation and I gloried in her courage. I resolved she should be my wife if she would accept me, which she did, and I have never regretted my choice and I think that I have had as happy a life as usually falls to the lot of mortals."

Chapter XVII

"Papa," said Laura Lasette, "all the girls have had graduating parties except Annette and myself. Would it not be nice for me to have a party and lots of fun, and then my birthday comes next week; now wouldn't it be just the thing for me to have a party?"

"It might be, darling, for you, but how would it be for me who would have to foot the bill?"

"Well, papa, could you not just give me a check like you do mama sometimes?"

"But mama knows how to use it."

"But papa, don't I know how also?"

"I have my doubts on that score, but let me refer you to your mother. She is queen of this realm, and in household matters I as a loyal subject, abide by her decisions."

"Well, I guess mama is all right on this subject."

Mrs. Lasette was perfectly willing to gratify her daughter, and it was decided to have an entertainment on Laura's birthday.

The evening of Mrs. Lasette's entertainment came bringing with it into her pleasant parlors a bright and merry throng of young people. It was more than a mere pleasure party. It was here that rising talent was encouraged, no matter how humble the garb of the possessor, and Mrs. Lasette was a model hostess who would have thought her entertainment a failure had any one gone from it smarting under a sense of social neglect. Shy and easily embarrassed Annette who was very seldom invited anywhere, found herself almost alone in that gay and chattering throng. Annette was seated next to several girls who laughed and chatted incessantly with each other without deigning to notice her. Mrs. Lasette entering the room with Mr. Luzerne whom she presented to the company, and noticing the loneliness and social isolation of Annette, gave him a seat beside her, and was greatly gratified that she had found the means to relieve the tedium of Annette's position. Mrs. Lasette had known him as a light hearted boy, full of generous impulses, with laughing eyes and a buoyant step, but he had been absent a number of years, and had developed into a handsome man with a magnificent physique, elegant in his attire, polished in his manners and brilliant in conversation. Just such a man as is desirable as a companion and valuable as a friend, staunch, honorable and true, and it was rumored that he was quite wealthy. He was generally cheerful, but it seemed at times as if some sad memories came over him, dashing all the sunshine from his face and leaving in its stead, a sadness which it was touching to behold. Some mystery seemed to surround his life, but being reticent in reference to his past history, there was a dignity in his manner which repelled all intrusion into the secrecy over which he choose to cast a veil. Annette was not beautiful, but her face was full of expression and her manner winsome at times. Lacking social influence and social adaptation, she had been ignored in society, her faults of temper made prominent her most promising traits of character left unnoticed, but this treatment was not without some benefit to Annette. It threw her more entirely on her own resources. At first she read when she had leisure, to beguile her lonely hours, and fortunately for her, she was directed in her reading by Mrs. Lasette, who gave and lent her books, which appealed to all that was highest and best in her nature, and kindled within her a lofty enthusiasm to make her life a blessing to the world. With such an earnest purpose, she was not prepared to be a social favorite in any society whose chief amusement was gossip, and whose keenest weapon was ridicule.

Mr. Luzerne had gone to Mrs. Lasette's with the hope of meeting some of the best talent in A.P., and had come to the conclusion that there was more lulliancy than depth in the intellectual life with which he came in contact; he felt that it lacked earnestness, purpose and grand enthusiasms and he was astonished to see the social isolation of Annette, whose society had interested and delighted him, and after parting with her he found his mind constantly reverting to her and felt grateful to Mrs. Lasette for affording him a rare and charming pleasure. Annette sat alone in her humble room with a new light in her eyes and a sense of deep enjoyment flooding her soul. Never before had she met with such an interesting and congenial gentleman. He seemed to understand as scarcely as any one else had done or cared to do. In the eyes of other guests she had been treated as if too insignificant for notice, but he had loosened her lips and awakened within her a dawning sense of her own ability, which others had chilled and depressed. He had fingered the keys of her soul and they had vibrated in music to his touch. Do not smile, gentle reader, and say that she was very easily impressed, it may be that you have never known what it is to be hungry, not for bread, but for human sympathy, to live with those who were never interested in your joys, nor sympathized in your sorrows. To whom your coming gave no joy and your absence no pain. Since Annette had lost her grandmother, she had lived in an atmosphere of coldness and repression and was growing prematurely cold. Her heart was like a sealed fountain beneath whose covering the bright waters dashed and leaped in imprisoned boundary. Oh, blessed power of human love to lighten human suffering, well may we thank the giver of every good and perfect gift for the love which gladdens hearts, brightens homes and sets the solitary in the midst of families. Mr. Luzerne frequently saw Annette at the house of Mrs. Lasette and occasionally called at her uncle's, but there was an air of restraint in the social atmosphere which repressed and chilled him. In that home he missed the cordial freedom and genial companionship which he always found at Mrs. Lasette's but Annette's apparent loneliness and social isolation awakened his sympathy, and her bright intelligence and good character commanded his admiration and respect, which developed within him a deep interest for the lovely girl. He often spoke admiringly of her and never met her at church, or among her friends that he did not gladly avail himself of the opportunity of accompanying her home. Madame rumor soon got tidings of Mr. Luzerne's attentions to Annette and in a shout the tongues of the gossips of A.P. began to wag. Mrs. Larkins who had fallen heir to some money, moved out of Tennis court, and often gave pleasant little teas to her young friends, and as a well spread table was quite a social attraction in A.P., her gatherings were always well attended. After rumor had caught the news of Mr. Luzerne's interest in Annette, Mrs. Larkins had a social at her house to which she invited him, and a number of her young friends, but took pains to leave Annette out in the cold. Mr. Luzerne on hearing that Annette was slighted, refused to attend. At the supper table Annette's prospects were freely discussed.

"I expected that Mr. Luzerne would have been here this evening, but he sent an apology in which he declined to come."

"Did you invite Annette?" said Miss Croker.

"No, I did not. I got enough of her when I lived next door to her."

"Well that accounts for Mr. Luzerne's absence. They remind me of the Siamese twins; if you see one, you see the other."

"How did she get in with him?"

"She met him at Mrs. Lasette's party, and he seemed so taken up with her that for a while he had neither eyes nor ears for any one else."

"That girl, as quiet as she looks, is just as deep as the sea."

"It is not that she's so deep, but we are so shallow. Miss Booker and Miss Croker were sitting near Annette and not noticing her, and we girls were having a good time in the corner to ourselves, and Annette was looking so lonely and embarrassed I think Mr. Luzerne just took pity on her and took especial pains to entertain her. I just think we stepped our feet into it by slighting Annette, and of course, as soon as we saw him paying attention to her, we wouldn't change and begin to make much of her."

"I don't know what he sees in Annette with her big nose and plain face."

"My father," said Laura Lasette, "says that Annette is a credit to her race and my mother is just delighted because Mr. Luzerne is attracted to her, but, girls, had we not better be careful how we talk about her? People might say that we are jealous of her and we know that we are taught that jealousy is as cruel as the grave."

"We don't see anything to be jealous about her. She is neither pretty nor stylish."

"But my mother says she is a remarkable girl," persisted Laura.

"Your mother," said Mrs. Larkins, "always had funny notions about Annette, and saw in her what nobody else did."

"Well, for my part, I hope it will be a match."

"It is easy enough for you to say so, Laura. You think it is a sure thing between you and Charley Cooper, but don't be too sure; there's many a slip between the cup and the lip."

There was a flush on Laura's cheek as she replied, "If there are a thousand slips between the cup and the lip and Charlie and I should never marry, let me tell you that I would almost as soon court another's husband as a girl's affianced lover. I can better afford to be an old maid than to do a dishonorable thing."

"Well, Laura, you are a chip off the old block; just like your mother, always ready to take Annette's part."

"I think, Mrs. Larkins, it is the finest compliment you can pay me, to tell me that I am like my dear mother."

Chapter XVIII

"Good morning," said Mr. Luzerne, entering Mr. Thomas' office. "Are you busy?"

"Not very; I had just given some directions to my foreman concerning a job I have undertaken, and had just settled down to read the paper. Well how does your acquaintance with Miss Harcourt prosper? Have you popped the question yet?"

"No, not exactly; I had been thinking very seriously of the matter, but I have been somewhat shaken in my intention."

"How so," said Mr. Thomas, laying down his paper and becoming suddenly interested.

"You know that I have had an unhappy marriage which has overshadowed all my subsequent life, and I cannot help feeling very cautious how I risk, not only my own, but another's happiness in a second marriage. It is true that I have been thinking of proposing to Miss Harcourt and I do prefer her to any young lady I have ever known; but there is a depreciatory manner in which people speak of her, that sorely puzzles me. For instance, when I ask some young ladies if they know Annette, they shrug their shoulders, look significantly at each other and say, 'Oh, yes, we know her; but she don't care for anything but books; oh she is so self conceited and thinks she knows more than any one else.' But when I spoke to Mrs. Larkins about her, she said Annette makes a fine appearance, but all is not gold that glitters. By this time my curiosity was excited, and I asked, 'What is the matter with Miss Harcourt? I had no idea that people were so ready to pick at her.' She replied, 'No wonder; she is such a spitfire.'"

"Well," said Mr. Thomas, a little hotly, "if Annette is a spitfire, Mrs. Larkins is a lot of combustion. I think of all the women I know, she has the greatest genius for aggravation. I used to board with her, but as I did not wish to be talked to death I took refuge in flight."

"And so you showed the white feather that time."

"Yes, I did, and I could show it again. I don't wonder that people have nick-named her 'Aunty talk forever.' I have known Annette for years and I known that she is naturally quick tempered and impulsive, but she is not malicious and implacable and if I were going to marry to-morrow I would rather have a quick, hot-tempered woman than a cold, selfish one, who never thought or cared about anyone but herself. Mrs. Larkins' mouth is not a prayer-book; don't be uneasy about anything she says against Annette."

Reassured by Mr. Thomas, Clarence Luzerne decided that he would ask Dr. Harcourt's permission to visit his niece, a request which was readily granted and he determined if she would consent that she should be his wife. He was wealthy, handsome and intelligent; Annette was poor and plain, but upright in character and richly endowed in intellect, and no one imagined that he would pass by the handsome and stylish girls of A.P. to bestow his affections on plain, neglected Annette. Some of the girls who knew of his friendship for Annette, but who never dreamed of its termination in marriage would say to Annette, "Speak a good word for me to Mr. Luzerne;" but Annette kept her counsel and would smile and think: I will speak a good word for myself. Very pleasant was the growing friendship between Annette and Mr. Luzerne. Together they read and discussed books and authors and agreed with wonderful unanimity, which often expressed itself in the words:

"I think as you do." Not that there was any weak compliance for the sake of agreement, but a unison of thought and feeling between them which gave a pleasurable zest to their companionship.

"Miss Annette," said Luzerne, "do you believe that matches are made in heaven?"

"I never thought anything about it."

"But have you no theory on the subject?"

"Not the least; have you?"

"Yes; I think that every human soul has its counterpart, and is never satisfied till soul has met with soul and recognized its spiritual affinity."

"Affinity! I hate the word."

"Why?"

"Because I think it has been so wrongly used, and added to the social misery of the world."

"What do you think marriage ought to be?"

"I think it should be a blending of hearts, an intercommunion of souls, a tie that only love and truth should weave, and nothing but death should part."

Luzerne listened eagerly and said, "Why, Miss Annette, you speak as if you had either loved or were using your fine imaginative powers on the subject with good effect. Have you ever loved any one?"

Annette blushed and stammered, and said, "I hardly know, but I think I have a fine idea of what love should be. I think the love of a woman for the companion of her future life should go out to him just as naturally as the waves leap to the strand, or the fire ascends to the sun."

"And this," said Luzerne, taking her hand in his, "is the way I feel towards you. Surely our souls have met at last. Annette," said he, in a voice full of emotion, "is it not so? May I not look on your hand as a precious possession, to hold till death us do part?"

"Why, Mr. Luzerne," said Annette, recovering from her surprise, "this is so sudden, I hardly know what to say. I have enjoyed your companionship and I confess have been pleased with your attentions, but I did not dream that you had any intentions beyond the enjoyment of the hour."

"No, Annette, I never seek amusement in toying with human hearts. I should deem myself a villain if I came into your house and stole your purse, and I should think myself no better if I entered the citadel of a woman's heart to steal her affections only to waste their wealth. Her stolen money I might restore, but what reparation could I make for wasted love and blighted affections? Annette, let there be truth between us. I will give you time to think on my proposal, hoping at the same time that I shall find favor in your eyes."

After Mr. Luzerne left, Annette, sat alone by the fireside, a delicious sense of happiness filling her soul with sudden joy. Could it be that this handsome and dignified man had honored her above all the girls in A.P., by laying his heart at her feet, or was it only a dream from which would come a rude awakening? Annette looked in the glass, but no stretch of imagination could make her conceive that she was beautiful in either form or feature. She turned from the glass with a faint sigh, wishing for his sake that she was as beautiful as some of the other girls in A.P., whom he had overlooked, not thinking for one moment that in loving her for what she was in intellect and character he had paid her a far greater compliment than if she had been magnificently beautiful and he had only been attracted by an exquisite form and lovely face. In a few days after Mr. Luzerne's proposal to Annette he came for the answer, to which he looked with hope and suspense.

"I am glad," he said, "to find you at home."

"Yes; all the rest of the family are out."

"Then the coast is clear for me?" There was tenderness and decision in his voice as he said, "Now, Annette, I have come for the answer which cannot fail to influence all my future life." He clasped the little hand which lay limp and passive in his own. His dark, handsome eyes were bent eagerly upon her as if scanning every nook and corner of her soul. Her eye fell beneath his gaze, her hand trembled in his, tears of joy were springing to her eyes, but she restrained them. She withdrew her hand from his clasp; he looked pained and disappointed. "Have I been too hasty and presumptuous?"

Annette said no rather faintly, while her face was an enigma he did not know how to solve.

"Why did you release your hand and avert your eyes?"

"I felt that my will was succumbing to yours, and I want to give you an answer untrammeled and uncontrolled by your will."

Mr. Luzerne smiled, and thought what rare thoughtfulness and judgment she has evinced. How few women older than herself would have thought as quickly and as clearly, and yet she is no less womanly, although she seems so wise.

"What say you, my dear Annette, since I have released your hand. May I not hope to hold this hand as the most precious of all my earthly possessions until death us do part?"

Annette fixed her eyes upon the floor as if she were scanning the figures on the carpet. Her heart beat quickly as she timidly repeated the words, "Until death us do part," and placed her hand again in his, while an expression of love and tender trust lit up the mobile and expressive face, and Annette felt that his love was hers; the most precious thing on earth that she could call her own. The engagement being completed, the next event in the drama was preparation for the wedding. It was intended that the engagement should not be long. Together they visited different stores in purchasing supplies for their new home. How pleasant was that word to the girl, who had spent such lonely hours in the home of her uncle. To her it meant one of the brightest spots on earth and one of the fairest types of heaven. In the evening they often took pleasant strolls together or sat and chatted in a beautiful park near their future home. One evening as they sat quietly enjoying themselves Annette said, "How happened it that you preferred me to all the other girls in A. P.? There are lots of girls more stylish and better looking; what did you see in poor, plain me?" He laughingly replied:

"I chose you out from all the rest,
The reason was I loved you best."

"And why did you prefer me?" She answered quite archly:

"The rose is red, the violet's blue,
Sugar is sweet and so are you."

"I chose you because of your worth. When I was young, I married for beauty and I pierced my heart through with many sorrows."

"You been married?" said Annette with a tremor in her tones. "Why, I never heard of it before."

"Did not Mr. Thomas or Mrs. Lasette tell you of it? They knew it, but it is one of the saddest passages of my life, to which I scarcely ever refer. She, my wife, drifted from me, and was drowned in a freshet near Orleans."

"Oh, how dreadful, and I never knew it."

"Does it pain you?"

"No, but it astonishes me."

"Well, Annette, it is not a pleasant subject, let us talk of something else. I have not spoken of it to you before, but to-day, when it pressed so painfully upon my mind, it was a relief to me to tell you about it, but now darling dismiss it from your mind and let the dead past bury its dead."

Just then there came along where they were sitting a woman whose face bore traces of great beauty, but dimmed and impaired by lines of sorrow and disappointment. Just as she reached the seat where they were sitting, she threw up her hands in sudden anguish, gasped out, "Clarence! my long lost Clarence," and fell at his feet in a dead faint.

As Mr. Luzerne looked on the wretched woman lying at his feet, his face grew deathly pale. He trembled like an aspen and murmured in a bewildered tone, "has the grave restored its dead?"

But with Annette there was no time for delay. She chaffed, the rigid hands, unloosed the closely fitting dress, sent for a cab and had her conveyed as quickly as possible to the home for the homeless. Then turning to Luzerne, she said bitterly, "Mr. Luzerne, will you explain your encounter with that unfortunate woman?" She spoke as calmly as she could, for a fierce and bitter anguish was biting at her heartstrings. "What claim has that woman on you?"

"She has the claim of being my wife and until this hour I firmly believed she was in her grave." Annette lifted her eyes sadly to his; he calmly met her gaze, but there was no deception in his glance; his eyes were clear and sad and she was more puzzled than ever.

"Annette," said he, "I have only one favor to ask; let this scene be a secret between us as deep as the sea. Time will explain all. Do not judge me too harshly."

"Clarence," she said, "I have faith in you, but I do not understand you; but here is the carriage, my work at present is with this poor, unfortunate woman, whose place I was about to unconsciously supplant."

Chapter XIX

And thus they parted. All their air castles and beautiful chambers of imagery, blown to the ground by one sad cyclone of fate. In the city of A.P., a resting place was found for the stranger who had suddenly dashed from their lips the scarcely tasted cup of happiness. Mr. Luzerne employed for her the best medical skill he could obtain. She was suffering from nervous prostration and brain fever. Annette was constant in her attentions to the sufferer, and day after day listened to her delirious ravings. Sometimes she would speak of a diamond necklace, and say so beseechingly, "Clarence, don't look at me so. You surely can't think that I am guilty. I will go away and hide myself from you. Clarence, you never loved me or you would not believe me guilty."

But at length a good constitution and careful nursing overmastered disease, and she showed signs of recovery. Annette watched over her when her wild ravings sounded in her ears like requiems for the loved and cherished dead. Between her and the happiness she had so fondly anticipated, stood that one blighted life, but she watched that life just as carefully as if it had been the dearest life on earth she knew.

One day, as Annette sat by her bedside, she surmised from the look on her face that the wandering reason of the sufferer had returned. Beckoning to Annette she said "Who are you and where am I?"

Annette answered, "I am your friend and you are with friends."

"Poor Clarence," she murmured to herself; "more sinned against than sinning."

"My dear friend," Annette said very tenderly, "you have been very ill, and I am afraid that if you do not be very quiet you will be very sick again." Annette gently smoothed her beautiful hair and tried to soothe her into quietness. Rest and careful nursing soon wrought a wondrous change in Marie Luzerne, but Annette thoughtfully refrained from all reference to her past history and waited for time to unravel the mystery she could not understand, and with this unsolved mystery the match between her and Luzerne was broken off. At length, one day when Marie's health was nearly restored, she asked for writing materials, and said, "I mean to advertise for my mother in a Southern paper. It seems like a horrid dream that all I knew or loved, even my husband, whom I deserted, believed that I was dead, till I came suddenly on him in the park with a young lady by his side. She looked like you. Was it you?"

"Yes," said Annette, as a sigh of relief came to her lips. If Clarence had wooed and won her he had not willfully deceived her. "Oh, how I would like to see him. I was wayward and young when I left him in anger. Oh, if I have sinned I have suffered; but I think that I could die content if I could only see him once more." Annette related the strange sad story to her physician, who decided that it was safe and desirable that there should be an interview between them. Luzerne visited his long lost wife and after a private interview, he called Annette to the room, who listened sadly while she told her story, which exonerated Luzerne from all intent to deceive Annette by a false marriage while she had a legal claim upon him.

"I was born," she said, "in New Orleans. My father was a Spaniard and my mother a French Creole. She was very beautiful and my father met her at a French ball and wished her for his companion for life, but as she was an intelligent girl and a devout Catholic she would not consent to live a life by which she would be denied the Sacrament of her Church; so while she could not contract a civil marriage, which would give her the legal claims of a wife, she could enter into an ecclesiastical marriage by which she would not forfeit her claim to the rights and privileges of the Church as a good Catholic. I was her only child, loved and petted by my father, and almost worshipped by my mother, and I never knew what it was to have a wish unfilled if it was in her power to gratify it. When I was about 16 I met Clarence Luzerne. People then said that I was very beautiful. You would scarcely think so now, but I suppose he thought so, too. In a short time we were married, and soon saw that we were utterly unfitted to each other; he was grave and I was gay; he was careful and industrious, I was careless and extravagant; he loved the quiet of his home and books; I loved the excitements of pleasure and the ball room, and yet I think he loved me, but it was as a father might love a wayward child whom he vainly tried to restrain. I had a cousin who had been absent from New Orleans a number of years, of whose antecedents I knew not scarcely anything. He was lively, handsome and dashing. My husband did not like his society, and objected to my associating with him. I did not care particularly for him, but I chafed against the restraint, and in sheer waywardness I continued the association. One day he brought me a beautiful diamond necklace which he said he had obtained in a distant land. I laid it aside intending to show it to my husband; in the meantime, a number of burglaries had been committed in the city of B., and among them was a diamond necklace. My heart stood still with sudden fear while I read of the account and while I was resolving what to do, my husband entered the house followed by two officers, who demanded the necklace. My husband interfered and with a large sum of money obtained my freedom from arrest. My husband was very proud of the honor of his family and blamed me for staining its record. From that day my husband seemed changed in his feelings towards me. He grew cold, distant and abstracted, and I felt that my presence was distasteful to him. I could not enter into his life and I saw that he had no sympathy with mine, and so in a fit of desperation I packed my trunk and took with me some money I had inherited from my father and left, as I said in a note, forever. I entered a convent and resolved that I would devote myself to the service of the poor and needy, for life had lost its charms for me. I had scarcely entered the convent before the yellow fever broke out and raged with fearful intensity. I was reckless of my life and engaged myself as a nurse. One day there came to our hospital a beautiful girl with a wealth of raven hair just like mine was before I became a nurse. I nursed her through a tedious illness and when she went out from the hospital, as I had an abundance of clothing, I supplied her from my wardrobe with all she needed, even to the dress she wore away. The clothing was all marked with my name. Soon after I saw in the paper that a young woman who was supposed from the marks on her clothing and the general description of her person to be myself was found drowned in a freshet. I was taken ill immediately afterwards and learned on recovering that I had been sick and delirious for several weeks. I sought for my mother, inquired about my husband, but lost all trace of them both till I suddenly came across my husband in Brightside Park. But Clarence, if you have formed other ties don't let me come between you and the sunshine. You are free to apply for a divorce; you can make the plea of willful desertion. I will not raise the least straw in your way. I will go back to the convent and spend the rest of my life in penitence and prayer. I have sinned; it is right that I should suffer." Clarence looked eagerly into the face of Annette; it was calm and peaceful, but in it he read no hope of a future reunion.

"What say you, Annette, would you blame me if I accepted this release?"

"I certainly would. She is your lawful wife. In the church of her father you pledged your faith to her, and I do not think any human law can absolve you from being faithful to your marriage vows. I do not say it lightly. I do not think any mother ever laid her first born in the grave with any more sorrow than I do to-day when I make my heart the sepulchre in which I bury my first and only love. This, Clarence, is the saddest trial of my life. I am sadder to-day than when I stood a lonely orphan over my grandmother's grave, and heard the clods fall on her coffin and stood lonely and heart-stricken in my uncle's house, and felt that I was unwelcome there. But, Clarence, the great end of life is not the attainment of happiness but the performance of duty and the development of character. The great question is not what is pleasant but what is right."

"Annette, I feel that you are right; but I am too wretched to realize the force of what you say. I only know that we must part, and that means binding my heart as a bleeding sacrifice on the altar of duty."

"Do you not know who drank the cup of human suffering to its bitter dregs before you? Arm yourself with the same mind, learn to suffer and be strong. Yes, we must part; but if we are faithful till death heaven will bring us sweeter rest." And thus they parted. If Luzerne had felt any faltering in his allegiance to duty he was too honorable and upright when that duty was plainly shown to him to weakly shrink from its performance, and as soon as his wife was able to travel he left A.P., for a home in the sunny South. After Luzerne had gone Annette thought, "I must have some active work which will engross my mind and use every faculty of my soul. I will consult with my dear friend Mrs. Lasette."

All unnerved by her great trial, Annette rang Mrs. Lasette's front door bell somewhat hesitatingly and walked wearily into the sitting-room, where she found Mrs. Lasette resting in the interval between twilight and dark. "Why Annette!" she said with pleased surprise, "I am so glad to see you. How is Clarence? I thought you would have been married before now. I have your wedding present all ready for you."

"Mrs. Lasette," Annette said, while her voice trembled with inexpressible sorrow, "it is all over."

Mrs. Lasette was lighting the lamp and had not seen Annette's face in the dusk of the evening, but she turned suddenly around at the sound of her voice and noticed the wan face so pitiful in its expression of intense suffering.

"What is the matter, my dear; have you and Luzerne had a lover's quarrel?"

"No," said Annette, sadly, and then in the ears of her sympathizing friend she poured her tale of bitter disappointment. Mrs. Lasette folded the stricken girl to her heart in tenderest manner.

"Oh, Mrs. Lasette," she said, "you make me feel how good it is for girls to have a mother."

"Annette, my brave, my noble girl, I am so glad."

"Glad of what, Mrs. Lasette?"

"Glad that you have been so true to conscience and to duty; glad that you have come through your trial like gold tried in the fiercest fire; glad that my interest in you has not been in vain, and that I have been able to see the blessed fruitage of my love and labors. And now, my dear child, what next?"

"I must have a change; I must find relief in action. I feel so weak and bruised in heart."

"A bruised reed will not break," murmured Mrs. Lasette to herself.

"Annette," said Mrs. Lasette, "this has been a fearful trial, but it must not be in vain; let it bring you more than happiness; let it bring you peace and blessedness. There is only one place for us to bring our sins and our sorrows, and that is the mercy seat. Let us both kneel there to-night and ask for grace to help in this your time of need. We are taught to cast our care upon Him for he careth for us. Come, my child, with the spirit of submission and full surrender, and consecrate your life to his service, body, soul and spirit, not as a dead offering, but a living sacrifice."

Together they mingled their prayers and tears, and when Annette rose from her knees there was a look of calmness on her face, and a deep peace had entered her soul. The strange trial was destined to bring joy and gladness and yield the peaceable fruit of righteousness in the future. Mrs. Lasette wrote to some friends in a distant Southern town where she obtained a situation for Annette as a teacher. Here she soon found work to enlist her interest and sympathy and bring out all the activity of her soul. She had found her work and the people among whom she labored had found their faithful friend.

Chapter XX

Luzerne's failure to marry Annette and re-instatement of his wife was the sensation of the season. Some pitied Annette; others blamed Luzerne, but Annette found, as a teacher, opportunity among the freedmen to be a friend and sister to those whose advantages had been less than hers. Life had once opened before her like a fair vision enchanted with delight, but her beautiful dream had faded like sun rays mingling with the shadows of night. It was the great disappointment of her life, but she roused up her soul to bear suffering and to be true to duty, and into her soul came a joy which was her strength. Little children learned to love her, the street gamins knew her as their friend, aged women blessed the dear child as they called her, who planned for their comfort when the blasts of winter were raging around their homes. Before her great trial she had found her enjoyment more in her intellectual than spiritual life, but when every earthly prop was torn away, she learned to lean her fainting head on Christ the corner-stone and the language of her heart was "Nearer to thee, e'en though it be a cross that raiseth me." In surrendering her life she found a new life and more abundant life in every power and faculty of her soul.

Luzerne went South and found Marie's mother who had mourned her child as dead. Tenderly they watched over her, but the seeds of death were sown too deeply in her wasted frame for recovery, and she wasted away and sank into a premature grave, leaving Luzerne the peaceful satisfaction of having smoothed her passage to the grave, and lengthened with his care, her declining days. Turning from her grave he plunged into active life. It was during the days of reconstruction when tricksters and demagogues were taking advantage of the ignorance and inexperience of the newly enfranchised citizens. Honorable and upright, Luzerne preserved his integrity among the corruptions of political life. Men respected him too much to attempt to swerve him from duty for personal advantage. No bribes ever polluted his hands, nor fraud, nor political chicanery ever stained his record.

He was the friend and benefactor of his race, giving them what gold is ever too poor to buy—the benefit of a good example and a noble life, and earned for himself the sobriquet by which he was called, "honest Luzerne." And yet at times he would turn wistfully to Annette and the memory of those glad, bright days when he expected to clasp hands with her for life. At length his yearning had become insatiable and he returned to A. P.

Laura Lasette had married Charley Cooper who by patience and industry had obtained a good position in the store of a merchant who was manly enough to let it be known that he had Negro blood in his veins, but that he intended to give him a desk and place in his establishment and he told his employees that he intended to employ him, and if they were not willing to work with him they could leave. Charley was promoted just the same as others according to his merits. Time had dealt kindly with Mrs. Lasette, as he scattered his silvery crystals amid her hair, and of her it might be said,

> Each silver hair, each wrinkle there
>   Records some good deed done,
> Some flower she scattered by the way
>   Some spark from love's bright sun.

Mrs. Larkins had grown kinder and more considerate as the years passed by. Mr. Thomas had been happily married for several years. Annette was still in her Southern home doing what she could to teach, help and befriend those on whose chains the rust of ages had gathered. Mr. Luzerne found out Annette's location and started Southward with a fresh hope springing up in his heart.

It was a balmy day in the early spring when he reached the city where Annette was teaching. Her home was a beautiful place of fragrance and flowers. Groups of young people were gathered around their teacher listening eagerly to a beautiful story she was telling them. Elderly women were scattered in little companies listening to or relating some story of Annette's kindness to them and their children.

"I told her," said one, "that I had a vision that some one who was fair, was coming to help us. She smiled and said she was not fair. I told her she was fair to me."

"I wish she had been here fifteen years ago," said another one. "Before she came my boy was just as wild as a colt, but now he is jist as stiddy as a judge."

"I just think," said another one, "that she has been the making of my Lucy. She's just wrapped up in Miss Annette, thinks the sun rises and sets in her." Old mothers whose wants had been relieved, came with the children and younger men too, to celebrate Annette's 31st birthday. Happy and smiling, like one who had passed through suffering into peace she stood, the beloved friend of old and young, when suddenly she heard a footstep on the veranda which sent the blood bounding in swift currents back to her heart and left her cheek very pale. It was years since she had heard the welcome rebound of that step, but it seemed as familiar to her as the voice of a loved and long lost friend, or a precious household word, and before her stood, with slightly bowed form and hair tinged with gray, Luzerne. Purified through suffering, which to him had been an evangel of good, he had come to claim the love of his spirit. He had come not to separate her from her cherished life work, but to help her in uplifting and helping those among whom her lot was cast as a holy benediction, and so after years of trial and pain, their souls had met at last, strengthened by duty, purified by that faith which works by love, and fitted for life's highest and holiest truths.

And now, in conclusion, permit me to say under the guise of fiction, I have essayed to weave a story which I hope will subserve a deeper purpose than the mere amusement of the hour, that it will quicken and invigorate human hearts and not fail to impart a lesson of usefulness and value.

Notes

1. In the original, this sentence reads: "After she became a wife and mother, instead of becoming entirely absorbed in a round of household cares and duties, and she often said, that the moment the crown of motherhood fell upon her how that she had poured a new interest in the welfare of her race."

2. The original reads "But Mr. Thompson."

3. The original reads "but during her short sojourn in the South."

4. In the original this sentence reads: "Young men anxious for places in the gift of government found that by winking at Frank Miller's vices and conforming to the demoralizing customs of his place, were the passports to political favors, and lacking moral stamina, hushed their consciences and became partakers of his sins."

5. The original reads "Mrs. Larking."

6. The original reads "said Mrs. Larkins, seating herself beside Mrs. Larking."

7. The original reads "continued Mr. Slocum."

8. The original reads "'Isn't your name Benny?'"

9. The original reads "said Charley Hastings."

10. The original reads "scarcely on intellect."

11. The original reads "expensive views."

12. The original reads "Mrs. Harcourt."

13. The original reads "Mrs. Hanson."

14. The original reads "Mr. Thomas."

15. The original reads "Tom Hanson."

Milton Keynes UK
Ingram Content Group UK Ltd.
UKHW030945071024
449371UK00016B/618